CALL CENTER CONNECTIONS

KEYS TO PRODUCE SUCCESSFUL CUSTOMER
SERVICE OUTCOMES

CALL CENTER SUCCESS SERIES

PETER DEHAAN

To all my many friends and colleagues in the call center industry

SERIES BY PETER LYLE DEHAAN

Call Center Success Series

Join call center veteran Peter Lyle DeHaan, PhD as he shares a lifetime of industry experience to help readers operate their call centers with increased effectiveness, produce greater success, and generate long-term profitability.

Sticky Series

The Sticky Series of career development books breaks down key business strategies in a coherent story-driven process to highlight what works and what doesn't. Through personal stories and eye-opening insights, Peter shares how readers can more effectively produce long-term results and increase their workplace fulfillment.

Be the first to hear about Peter's new books and receive updates at peterlyledehaan.com/newsletter.

CONTENTS

ARE YOU IN OR OUT?

UNDERSTAND INDUSTRY NUANCES

Since you're reading this book, you're *in* the call center industry. Yet the question, "Are you in or out?" doesn't ask about your connection to the industry, but rather your operation's role within it, relative to the greater call center industry.

Forgive me if you already know the answer, but too many people—even if they know their call center's role—don't have a comprehensive industry view. Here are the basics to get us started.

We classify call center activity in two ways. The first is if they handle *in*bound traffic or *out*bound traffic. The second is whether they are an *in*-house or *out*source operation. Therefore, "Are you in or out?" implies two questions. This produces four possible outcomes:

1) An *in*-house call center, doing *in*bound work

2) An *in*-house call center, doing *out*bound work

3) An *out*source call center, doing *in*bound work

4) An *out*source call center, doing *out*bound work

Inbound or Outbound?

Inbound or outbound refers to the direction of calls. That is, whether the center makes calls (outbound) or receives calls (inbound). For an outsider—or even an uninformed insider—this would seem to be a small distinction. "What's the big difference?" they ask. "Both involve agents, use phones, and are supported by technology. If you're doing one, the other should be no problem."

Not so fast. The differences are as profound as day and night.

Inbound: Since inbound call centers answer calls, agents work in a reactive mode. That is, they wait for the phone to ring (or for the next call to drop from the queue) and then they react to it.

Inbound call centers are equipped with ACDs (automatic call distribution) to send calls to the *next available agent*. Inbound operations are staffed more hours of the day than their outbound counterparts, with most operating 24/7. Agents are scheduled to work in anticipation of projected call volume based on historical data, future projections, and marketing initiatives.

Outbound: For the outbound call center, agents must be proactive. That is, they need to take initiative. The successful outbound agent has a different personality than the ideal inbound agent. Even if the nature of their outbound work is not specifically in sales, they still need a sales mentality. They need to engage the called party, lead them toward a stated objective, and deal well with rejection —some of which may be personally directed.

Outbound call centers rely on predictive dialers to place calls. Outbound centers have reduced hours of operation, limited by law and the needs of specific campaigns. In this situation, agents are scheduled as needed to complete a requisite number of calls within a certain window of time.

Outbound call centers must comply with national and state laws that regulate (that is, limit) outbound calling, historically called telemarketing. When these laws were implemented, it greatly curtailed outbound calling and forced marginal players out of the industry. Most that remain are professional operations, providing a valuable service.

Blended: Not to be overlooked, the concept of blended call centers (those doing both inbound and outbound work) has been pursued, although with varying degrees of success. Blending can occur at different levels.

The first is within a call center, where some agents are answering calls while others are placing calls.

The second level of blending occurs with agents who are

proficient with both calling disciplines. They can be scheduled for either activity as needed. Most agents cannot successfully make this transition from one day to the next, but those who can appreciate the variety.

The third level of blending occurs from call to call. If an unexpected rush of incoming calls occurs, the outbound reps are automatically removed from the agent pool of the predictive dialer and placed into the agent pool for the ACD. This continues until the rush ends and the process reverses. Conversely, if it's a slow day for incoming calls, these agents can be automatically switched to the outbound campaign. While this type of efficiency excites upper management, it often works better on paper than in reality. Reps who can successfully handle this type of on-the-fly mental adjustment are rare.

In-House or Outsource?

While the concepts of inbound and outbound are generally understood, the terms in-house and outsource cause some confusion. An in-house call center is one where the work done is performed for the company itself—that is, internally —and is generally secondary to the main function of the company and the products or services they produce.

Conversely, an outsource call center provides call center services to other companies. Phone work is all they do; it's their business.

In-House: There are arguably 50,000 to 100,000 call centers in the United States. The range is so great because they are sometimes challenging to identify. Of these, most are in-house operations.

Outsource: Outsource call centers, though a minority, are increasing in number and importance. This trend is due to more and more companies looking to outsourcing to increase service levels or options, return to their core competencies, save money, or all three.

At outsource call centers, processing calls is all they do. Therefore, they must do it well and cost-effectively if they are to remain viable. They also enjoy an economy-of-scale not feasible for most in-house operations. As such, their margins allow the client to save money and the outsource call center to make money.

The outsource call center industry traces its beginnings to the post-World War I era, when enterprising telephone answering services begin popping up around the country. Even though the label would follow decades later, these entrepreneurs were, in fact, the first outsource call centers. The modern era of outsource call centers began in the 1980s, when the introduction of toll-free numbers made it cost-effective to centralize call centers. Still, it wasn't until more recently that the outsourcing label was applied.

Outsource call centers are similar in design and function to their in-house counterparts. There are, however, a few important distinctions.

First, while an in-house call center can be viewed as either a cost-center or a profit-center, the outsource call center must be a profit-center and is often the only source of revenue for the company.

Second, the outsource call center must continually search for and find new clients to serve. Therefore, it has an external sales and marketing aspect that is not needed at in-house call centers.

Last, in-house call centers service their company's customers, whereas the outsource call center serves their clients' customers. Therefore, agents at an outsource call center work *for* their clients, but they work *with* their clients' customers or prospects.

Outsource is Not Synonymous with Offshore

There was a trend to move call center activity to other countries that boast stable technological infrastructures and offer qualified workers who possess lower wage expectations. This is offshore outsourcing, but it is too often wrongly shortened to outsourcing.

This is incorrect shorthand, as the majority of U.S. call center outsourcing is, and will continue to be, to U.S.-based call centers. Offshore outsourcing, which is getting all the attention, is a small minority of the total call center outsource picture. Although offshore outsourcing will continue to occur, some companies have tried offshoring and then pulled back in disappointment when it failed to deliver the expected results.

Moving Forward

Whether your call center is inbound or outbound, in-house or outsource, this book is for you.

OPERATIONS AND MANAGEMENT

We'll begin our discussion of call center success by looking at considerations that fall under the general umbrella of "operations and management."

With these chapters as our backdrop, we'll then use them as a foundation to delve into specific areas in upcoming sections.

Let's get started on this exciting journey.

ANSWERING THE CALL IS JUST THE FIRST STEP

THE GOAL IS TO SERVE CALLERS

Companies once embraced a vision of providing online self-service, shutting down their call centers and staffed customer service offerings.

This didn't work as well as hoped, with companies moving away from forced self-service to some degree of customer service. It matters not if they offer customer service by telephone, text chat, or email. What's important is their attempt to provide support to customers and not let them flounder. This is good for consumers, companies, workers, and the contact center industry. Everyone wins.

While some companies hide their customer service channels behind a wall of self-service options and FAQs, others make their offerings prominent. They are the champions. They want to make it easy for customers and potential customers to reach them. They've figured out that it's good business to help the people who buy their products—the same folks who make it possible for them to stay in business.

Unfortunately, some companies try to control the method of contact. They still don't comprehend that the customer is important, but at least these businesses are doing something. Other companies limit their hours of availability. They decide they can't justify having customer service staff work on the third shift or outside regular business hours. News flash: Outsource the work to provide 24/7 coverage on a cost-effective basis.

Smart companies offer a full range of contact options: phone, chat, email, and even snail mail for those so inclined. And they offer them 24/7. I applaud them. They have the right vision and understand the importance of providing support to their current customers and prospective buyers.

Yet this is only the beginning. Answering the phone, accepting a chat request, or reading an email is just the first step. It's a critical step, to be sure, but execution makes the difference.

Final Thoughts

I commend companies for answering their phone. The next step is to help the people who contact them. That's the key to good customer service.

IS YOUR MANAGEMENT STYLE HURTING YOUR CALL CENTER?

AFTER DOING ALL YOU CAN TO HIRE STAFF, TURN YOUR ATTENTION TOWARD RETENTION

A college friend shared his experience working at his part-time job. Several of his coworkers had quit, and he planned to do so as well. His departure would move his employer from drastically short-staffed to critically understaffed. She begged him to stay and offered him a significant pay bump, moving him to nearly three times the minimum wage for his unskilled, entry-level position.

He accepted, but he quickly regretted his decision.

Three weeks later he quit for good. "She was just too hard to work for," he said, "and no amount of money would get me to stay."

He found another job right away. Though his new one doesn't pay as well, he likes his boss and feels appreciated.

He now enjoys going to work. As a bonus, the hours don't interfere with his school schedule or studying.

In a different era, his first boss's management style would have worked. Yes, she would have churned through employees, but hiring a replacement wouldn't have been an issue.

Times have changed. It seems every business today is in a hiring mode. They've upped their pay, improved their compensation plan, and lowered their expectations. But they still have trouble filling open slots, as well as keeping the employees they do have. And some of the employees they have fall short of expectations and are less than the caliber they once hired.

The common solutions to filling open positions in a tight labor market are to pay more, improve benefits, and be more accommodating. These are good solutions, but a better approach may be to re-examine your management style.

Quite succinctly, is your management style hurting your call center?

In thinking back to past jobs, I've had managers who were patient, and others who were demanding. Some were kind, and others were tyrants. A few were complimentary, and others were condemning. I liked some and feared others. And when it came to compensation, some were fair, and others were cheap.

For the good jobs with great bosses, I stayed with those companies for a long time, working for them until my situation changed. For the jobs with less-than-ideal bosses, I moved on as quickly as I could.

Each one of these was a learning opportunity, teaching me what to do and not to do when it came to supervising staff and leading people.

When I moved into management, I strived to be a fair boss and treat employees well—to be the kind of employer I wanted to work for.

Though I didn't always succeed at meeting my goal, I know that most of the time I did. Some employees noticed this and even thanked me for it. And a few told me I was the best boss they ever had.

I'm not sure how much my focus on being a desirable boss and worthy employer affected our call center turnover, but I do know it helped. I also felt good about myself and the effort I put forth to make the operation a better place to work.

If your call center is short-staffed and you can't find enough qualified employees despite paying more and offering more, the long-term solution may be to focus on the retention side of the equation.

Final Thoughts

Look at your management style. Seek changes that will allow you to have a more positive impact on your staff and lead them in a more effective way.

RESPONDING TO CALL TRAFFIC FLUCTUATIONS

YOU CAN'T SCHEDULE FOR THE UNEXPECTED, BUT THAT'S NO EXCUSE TO BE UNPREPARED

T raffic at many inbound call centers fluctuates with the weather, affecting some operations more than others. Of course, non-weather-related events can also impact call traffic. This includes natural disasters, pandemics, threats of violence, and media-produced frenzies. The list goes on with as much variety as our imaginations can envision.

Although some traffic fluctuations occur with predictable regularity, other call traffic spurts strike with little warning. What's a call center to do? Here are some options to consider.

Handle It the Best You Can

The first impulse in responding to more traffic than you're prepared for is to work faster, cut nonessential tasks, and answer calls with greater intention. This helps . . . a bit . . . for a while. You may tap non-phone staff to put on a headset and get to work.

Cutting breaks and shortening lunches emerges as a tempting thought, but don't give in to that temptation. Asking staff to extend shifts and work overtime is another approach many call centers pursue. Sometimes this becomes mandatory. It helps to get calls answered, but employee morale takes a hit.

An optional strategy is to ignore the escalating number of calls in the queue and just process whatever calls you can while working at your normal pace. If the call is important, the caller will hold or call back later, at least you hope so. Regardless, customer satisfaction plummets.

Intentionally Overstaff

Given this situation, call center managers may intentionally overhire and overschedule. This provides a nice buffer to deal with traffic peaks and longer-term surges. The side effect of this well-intended strategy is that during times of normal traffic levels, you're either paying for unproductive work or your staff isn't getting as many hours as they wish. Neither outcome is a good one.

Throttle Incoming Calls

A third solution entertained by anxious call center managers is to reduce the number of incoming calls during high-traffic situations. One method is to provide a busy signal to callers. A second approach is to play a recording asking them to try later. A third possibility is to allow them to schedule a call-back. Of course, the callback solution requires that you're not still dealing with the high-traffic situation when it comes time to make that return phone call.

Overflow to Another Location

If you've concluded that the first three options aren't good ones, you're right. If your call center is part of a multiloca-tion operation, an easy solution is to send excess calls to another center in your network. For this to be a viable solu-tion, however, it requires that the other location is not suffering from the same malady.

Some multilocation call centers automatically route calls from one location to another based on incoming traffic and agent availability. In these cases, the overall traffic self-regu-lates, which means that unexpected high call volume coming into one center will impact all call centers in the network. Yet one underperforming center can drag down the entire group.

Outsource to Another Call Center

A final consideration is to outsource your overflow calls. Not only is this a great solution for high-traffic scenarios, but it also works well for understaffing. You can establish whatever events you want to trigger an overflow situation. It might be the number of calls in queue, the current wait time, or the number of abandons.

Select an outsource call center that's geographically distant from your location to reduce the risk of them suffering from the same scenario as your call center.

Final Thoughts

Though there's no ideal way to deal with unexpected call traffic, there are steps you can take to reduce the negative impact on both callers and staff. But don't wait until you're in the middle of a crisis to consider solutions. Plan now before you're swamped with calls.

THE IMPORTANCE OF CHANNEL CONSISTENCY

GIVE CUSTOMERS THE EXPERIENCE THEY EXPECT, REGARDLESS OF HOW THEY CONTACT YOU

W hat are your personal experiences when you contact a company? If your experiences match mine, you have more less-than-satisfactory encounters and few positive ones.

Now contrast your experiences with your own call center operation. How do you compare? Consider what you can do to ensure your callers don't undergo the same frustrations you endured.

Text Chat

As a consumer, I've never been a big fan of chat services. Though my typing speed is decent, my accuracy isn't. In addition, as a recovering perfectionist, I double-check and triple-check my words and their meaning before I click *send*. A phone call, assuming that option is available, seems so much more effective.

In addition, my past encounters with text chat were never good. Sometimes a rep never came online, other times the delay between responses was unbearable, and many times the rep never really answered my questions. Once, a response was completely off topic, and I made the mistake of typing, "Did you even read my question?" The rep's response wasn't kind. These experiences conditioned me to avoid text chat.

But things are changing—at least with some implementations. My recent text chat experiences have been better, approaching excellent. (I imagine hearing a collective sigh of relief from all of you who provide this service.) Each time I received the help I sought in a timely manner. The reps responded to my chat requests quickly and answered my questions fully, engaging me in the process.

One of the best came from a well-known computer company. I asked the rep how many simultaneous sessions she handled. Her answer was three, but she added, "Sometimes they ask us to handle four if we get busy." I doubt these requests are optional, but it was refreshing for her to use the word *ask* instead of *require*.

With artificial intelligence (AI) now providing bots to take the place of real people on text chat, I've seen text chat effectiveness deteriorate. Yet one company I interact with provided quick and accurate answers in four out of my last five sessions. This development gives me hope for text chat.

Phone

For most of my life, the telephone provided my preferred channel. Assuming I got a knowledgeable rep, I received my answer fast. And I had confidence in their reply.

More recently, the people I talk with are undertrained. This includes both product knowledge and customer service skills. I hope this trend doesn't continue, but I fear it will.

Email

I've now shifted to email as my preferred channel—at least for non-time-critical issues. With email, I can craft a concise query to ensure I correctly communicate my intent. A bonus is ending up with a documented response I can review later.

Channel Consistency

In contacting one company over a problem they caused, I interacted with them on all three channels: text, phone, and email. This company excelled with their text chat, disappointed with their phone service, and had an epic failure with email.

Their channel experiences didn't align. I judged them by

their weakest channels, not their best one. My three decades as their customer ended, largely because their weakest channel so disappointed me.

Final Thoughts

Look at your operation through the eyes of a customer. Then fix what you don't like.

CALL CENTER SHRINKAGE
THREE MUST-KNOW STAFFING METRICS

I n retail, the term shrinkage is euphemistically used to reference stock that *disappears* before it can be sold. It's a product the retailer bought but can't sell.

To be direct, shrinkage is theft. While some of this occurs in the form of shoplifting, it also happens when employees take products home or overlook coworkers who do. Regardless of the source or the motives, shrinkage hurts everyone in the form of higher consumer prices and lower company profits. This affects jobs and threatens the business's future viability.

Some retail operations take a surprisingly relaxed position about shrinkage, viewing it as an inevitable cost of doing business. Others see it as the theft that it is. They take aggressive steps to eliminate it—or at least reduce it.

Call Center Shrinkage

Shrinkage in the retail environment has an analogous application to the call center. A call center does not have tangible inventory that can disappear. A call center's inventory is human capital, that is, the call center schedule. Shrinkage in a call center, therefore, is agents who are *on the clock* but who aren't processing calls. This could be from agents who aren't at their stations when they should be, not being logged in, not being *in rotation*, or who employ some trick to block calls.

Similarly to retail, some call centers take a surprisingly relaxed position about this shrinkage of the schedule, also viewing it as an inevitable cost of doing business. Their response is intentional overstaffing. This only serves to cover the problem, not resolve the underlying cause.

Other call centers see shrinkage as little more than stealing—stealing time. Like their retail counterparts, they take aggressive steps to eliminate or at least reduce it. Call center shrinkage likewise hurts everyone: a lower service level to the customer, reduced profits to the company, and decreased employee morale.

There are three factors that help track, explain, and counter call center shrinkage. They are adherence, availability, and occupancy.

Adherence

Adherence is a measurement of the time agents are scheduled to work compared to the time they actually do. Why is adherence important? Quite simply, it's because the schedule was developed to match the traffic projection, and when the schedule is not fully worked, the result is understaffing. In an ideal situation, staff should adhere 100 percent to their schedules. Unfortunately, this seldom happens.

Adherence can be best tracked by comparing *logged in* time to scheduled time. Most call center managers are shocked the first time they look at this. It can represent a huge unnecessary cost to the call center, as well as contribute to lower service levels.

Several factors can account for differences between the schedule and the time worked. The first area is planned breaks, lunches, and training. This is the only acceptable contributor to adherence discrepancy. Depending on the length of breaks, the best resulting adherence will be around 90 percent. Forty-five minutes of breaks in an eight-hour shift will result in an adherence of 90.6 percent (7.25 hours out of 8).

The second consideration is absences, late arrivals, and early departures. Unless these openings are filled, the result is a disparity between the schedule and the fulfillment of that schedule. If this missed work is paid time off, such as paid sick time, then there is both a dollar cost and service impact that results.

The third area is unscheduled breaks or any other distraction that causes agents to leave their positions. When combining all these items, it isn't uncommon for call centers to have adherence rates around 75 percent, although well-run centers will be in the low 90s (as determined by their established break schedule).

Adherence is the first of three related scheduling metrics. The next is availability.

Availability

A second, and related, staffing metric is availability. Availability is a subset of adherence. Of the time that staff is adhering to their schedule, availability measures how much of that time they are ready—that is, *available*—to answer calls. It can be easily calculated by comparing available time (also called *on time*, *in rotation*, or *ready*) to logged in time.

Specifically, it's the percentage that results from dividing available time by logged in time. Although the ideal goal of 100 percent availability is achievable (that is, ready to process calls all the time agents are logged in), 98 to 99 percent is more realistic.

Agent availability is strictly within the control of agents. It's determined by each agent's willingness to keep his or her station in a state of readiness to be assigned calls. Simply put, it measures whether the agent is available to take calls all the time.

Availability is the second scheduling related metric. The third is occupancy.

Occupancy

Occupancy is the amount of time agents spend talking to callers compared to the time they are turned on or available. Although it is possible to have 100 percent occupancy, the corresponding service level would be poor. One hundred percent occupancy means agents are talking to callers the entire time they're logged in. It also means there are calls continuously in queue, waiting to be assigned as soon as an agent completes a call. The resulting efficiency is great, but callers can end up waiting in queue for several minutes and more. Therefore, 100 percent occupancy doesn't produce quality service and leads to agent fatigue and burnout.

Interestingly, ideal occupancy rates vary greatly with the size of the call center. Smaller centers can only achieve a low occupancy rate (perhaps around 25 percent) while maintaining an acceptable service level. Conversely, large call centers can realize a much higher occupancy rate (90 percent and higher) and still maintain that same service level.

This dynamic relationship between occupancy rates and call center size is the underlying impetus for mergers and acquisitions among outsource call centers and is a profound example of economies of scale. Call centers in the 10 to 20 seat range typically see occupancy rates around 50 percent.

To calculate occupancy, divide the total agent time (that is, talk time plus wrap-up time) by agent *on time*. Determine occupancy for each agent as well as for the entire operation.

Two Case Studies

Now, let's consider all three metrics together and apply them to two call centers: a well-run call center contrasted to a poorly managed one. We'll assume they're the same size and have a realized occupancy rate of 50 percent.

Call Center A has an adherence rate of 90 percent and an availability rate of 95 percent (along with the 50 percent occupancy rate). For each 8-hour shift there is 3.42 hours of on-line time or actual work (8 hours x 90 percent x 95 percent x 50 percent).

Call Center B has an adherence rate of 75 percent and an availability rate of 65 percent (with an occupancy rate of 50 percent). For each 8-hour shift there is only 1.8 hours of on-line time or actual work (8 hours x 75 percent x 60 percent x 50 percent).

Although the results for call center A, a well-run operation, may surprise, the corresponding number for call center B is shocking. In fact, to maintain the same service level, Call Center B would need to schedule almost twice (1.9 times) as many hours as Call Center A. Consider what a significant impact this would have on profits.

Lest you think that these are unrealistic numbers, both are real situations describing call centers where I served as a consultant. It takes a concerted and ongoing management effort to be like Call Center A, while all too many operations are more like Call Center B.

Final Thoughts

I challenge you to run your numbers to see how you compare—and then take steps to improve them.

Don't let call center shrinkage lead to profitability shrinkage!

THE FAST-FOOD FACTOR

DISCOVER A SIMPLE METHOD TO DETERMINE YOUR STARTING PAY

I've never met anyone who felt they were overpaid. Occasionally, someone will privately admit to being adequately compensated, but most people are quick to claim their pay falls short of what they deserve. This is especially true with call center agents.

I've experienced this repeatedly, both in running call centers and as an industry consultant. In either instance, agents view me as someone who can improve their pay rates, elevating paychecks to an appropriate level. What's perplexing is that it never matters what the pay rate is. The consistent belief among agents is that their pay is too low.

What Is an Appropriate Starting Wage?

Compensation is the single greatest expense a call center faces. It accounts for anywhere from 40 percent to 85 percent of a call center's total expenses, with the actual level being a factor of call center size and economies of scale.

But what is an appropriate rate of pay for call center agents? While employee compensation is an economic means by which they support themselves, in North America money is also an esteem factor workers use to measure their importance to their company, society, and family. Their self-esteem hinges on it. Although I object to money being a measure of their true worth, instead favoring things like character and integrity, our materialistic society warps our staff's priorities and skews their perspectives.

If agent compensation were an issue unto itself, there would be little need to worry about it. Merely pay agents what they ask. Obviously, it isn't this simple. Agent compensation is a tradeoff. Pay too little and turnover shoots up, training costs increase, and morale decreases. The ensuing turmoil causes quality to suffer and customers to complain. However, paying too much causes the outflow of money to exceed the inflow of cash. No company can stay in business if it continually loses money.

Companies need to find the delicate balance between seeking to maintain ongoing employment for agents at the possible risk of sub-standard pay or increasing pay at the risk of losing those same jobs when the company closes because it's no longer competitive.

Some managers attempt to back into appropriate pay rates. They apply an arbitrary labor percentage to their total revenue. Then they allocate the resulting dollars to the schedule that has been projected for their target service level. The resulting calculation is a mathematically derived hourly rate for their call center agents—and it is usually wrong.

A Simple Benchmark

It's always been my aim to pay an appropriate level of compensation to call center agents. Not too much as to jeopardize the future viability of the business, but not so low as to deprive staff of what they can and should earn. Again, that brings us back to the question of what is the appropriate rate? Fortunately, the answer is close to home and easy to determine. It resides in your local quick-serve restaurants. I call it the fast-food factor.

In explaining why restaurants can serve as a benchmark for starting labor rates, I don't want to appear disparaging toward their employees or the job they do. Yet many call centers compete with quick-serve restaurants to staff their operation.

Quite simply, if you hire call center agents at a fast-food wage, you get a fast-food mentality and a fast-food performance. Yes, you will find the occasional star employee, but how long do you expect to retain him or her?

What you will find is people with little or no work history who view the job as temporary, have little concept of customer service, and fail to comprehend the necessity of getting to work on time, much less the courtesy of giving two weeks' notice before quitting.

With the average agent training time exceeding the average employee tenure at a fast-food restaurant, you can't afford to hire someone who may quit before they complete training. Yet when you compete with fast-food restaurants for entry-level employees, this is the outcome you will achieve.

Some call center managers may emphatically assert that they can't afford to match what the local fast-food restaurant offers. Yes, you can—in fact, you must.

So, we have established the need to pay more than fast-food restaurants, but how much more? I've found that even paying a quarter an hour more can make a difference. Fifty cents to a dollar more will have a much larger and more profound effect—if you do it right.

What you must avoid, however, when raising your starting wage, is merely to make it easier to find the same caliber of people. You need to raise your standards and expectations too. When you pay more, you should expect more.

Two Case Studies

In working with one client, the staff kept complaining that "people who work fast-food earn more than we do." After the fifth such complaint, I needed to know the truth. I invested an hour and visited the seven fast-food restaurants within walking distance of the call center.

The staff's perception was wrong, but the misinformation had gone unchallenged and was repeated often enough that the fabrication had become accepted as true. Correcting the deception was the first step in countering low employee morale and quelling worker dissatisfaction. The second step was to implement a small adjustment to the starting wage to make a better distinction between the two types of jobs.

At another client's location, agents had a much higher starting wage, but they too complained of being undercompensated. Again, I did my quick survey and found their starting wage to be three dollars higher than the fast-food benchmark. No adjustment was needed.

Fortunately, accompanying this higher starting wage were tighter pre-employment screenings and elevated expectations. The caliber of the staff was noticeably greater than what I typically saw in call centers. True, the call center manager had a huge part in making this happen, but she couldn't have been successful had the organization's starting pay and hiring practices not provided her with the ability to hire quality people.

Final Thoughts

To determine the appropriate hourly rate for your call center agents, you have four options:

1. Continue what you are doing (which probably isn't working).
2. Pay someone thousands of dollars to do a "proper" wage study.
3. Refer to local wage surveys (which seldom list data for call center agents).
4. Spend an hour surveying your nearby quick-serve restaurants.

Applying the fast-food factor has never let me down and, I suspect, it won't let you down either.

WE CAN DO THAT

STANDARDIZATION VERSUS SPECIALIZATION

The Ford Model T automobile was produced in only one color. Supposedly, Henry Ford quipped, "You can have any color, as long as it's black."

By standardizing the manufacturing process, his assembly-line production method changed the way cars were made and introduced a predictable consistency. At the time, these traits were highly desirable and greatly applauded by the buying public.

Parallels to this are seen in call centers, where productivity and efficiency are the precise reasons for their creation. To best accomplish this, tasks must be able to be repeated with regular uniformity in a prescribed manner. Someone calling to order two left-handed widgets today should be handled the same as another person making an identical request of a different agent—be it today or next month.

Consistency—of both processes and results—is the watchword. To accomplish this, call centers established their own Standard Operating Procedure (SOP), with agents being trained to achieve this standard with consistency. All calls are answered in the same manner with a common phraseology, information is verified according to an established protocol, and calls end with a specified parting phrase.

This one-size-fits-all approach to providing call center services is the epitome of streamlined operations and cost-containment. These are great benefits to stakeholders, providing they can accept the call center's SOP.

When a department (for in-house operations) or a client (for outsource operations) places a *special order*, such as not using automation when it is part of a call center's SOP, the call center faces a dilemma.

Do you keep things standard to retain your operational efficacy, or do you allow for variations to meet departmental or client needs? At one time, virtually all call centers followed the Model T production model, with a one-size-fits-all mindset. Some still do, and there's nothing wrong with that—providing the ramifications are understood.

When you allow variations, mistakes can—and do—occur. The result is increased customer service issues, coupled with increased costs.

When every car was made the same way, there was

little chance of having it made incorrectly. With special orders, however, the potential for mistakes jumps. The same situation applies to call processing. In both cases, a procedure for dealing with errors must be established, along with the money to cover the cost of rectifying these problems.

Offering variations in service complicates training. When specific department or client requests are the exception, agents are trained on the SOP. Any special requests deviate from that standard and are dealt with separately— with special training, at an extra cost.

If departmental or client preferences are the norm, however, then agents are trained to expect and accommodate variability. In essence, the SOP becomes mass customization. This slows down call processing since the work for each step needs to be considered prior to acting. Even a fraction of a second delay, when compounded throughout the day, has huge implications.

Despite this, there are still generally some nonnegotiable items. This may be a result of infrastructure limitations (not having a requested technology), philosophical paradigms (certain things the call center will or will not do), or practical limitations (excessive errors that occur when attempting a particular exception).

In today's business environment, departments and clients expect you to accommodate them. Therefore, it's wise to oblige them whenever and however possible. To exemplify a positive can-do attitude, I used to tell my staff that whatever the client request, the answer is, "Yes, we can do that. Let me find out how much it will cost."

Final Thoughts

Consider if your call center should follow a standardization model or a specialization paradigm. Consider the up and downsides of each. Develop the appropriate SOP. Train staff accordingly.

DO YOU SURVEY YOUR CALLERS?

WHEN DONE RIGHT, SURVEYS PRODUCE GREAT VALUE

As a consumer, I have a love-hate reaction to surveys. Sometimes I dismiss them and feel guilty. Other times I take them and feel I've wasted my time. I group surveys into four categories:

Market Research

The first type of survey is market research. All those who complete the survey have a chance to win some great prize. I'm enticed by the possible reward, but most of the time I fall outside the target demographic, or the survey ends prematurely when I give an unacceptable response.

The reward never materializes. Because of this, I've stopped taking these surveys.

The Sales Call in Disguise

This ploy is a sales pitch posing as a survey. If you answer their questions correctly—that is, confirm yourself as a prospect—you earn yourself a sales pitch. These surveys, often presented as research, appeal to one's sense of duty or the opportunity to influence some important decision.

Companies have duped me enough times that I skip these surveys as well.

Subverted by Employees

After completing a transaction, the salesperson or customer service rep implores me to take their survey, usually in a most enthusiastic manner. Often they say—or at least imply—that if I fail to do so, they could get in trouble. Once I commit to participate, they then tell me what scores to give them. "Make sure you give me all fives," they say. "Anything less—even a four—is a failure." Their bonus, or even their job, is at stake. Will I help them?

Masterful at their plea, it's hard not to comply. But their effort to game the system disgusts me. My response is to threaten to give them all ones. My wife says that's a terrible thing to do. I say it's terrible for employees to skew the survey results.

The last time this happened, my wife took the survey to keep me from carrying out my threat.

Company Centric

The final type of survey also appears as a customer service evaluation, but when considering the questions, they seldom truly address customer issues.

Many common questions—such as hold time, speed to answer, first call resolution, agent courtesy, and so forth—appear to address customer service. The reality is that call centers can achieve these statistical goals yet still not provide optimum service to callers.

To counter this weakness, some surveys ask, "Based only on this call, would you recommend us to your friends?" Although this infers customer satisfaction at a basic level, it still falls short.

I doubt I would ever recommend a company based solely on one call. My enthusiasm, or lack thereof, comes from multiple interactions and the overall utility of a company's product or service. Each subsequent transaction moves my view up or down. One call cannot be considered in isolation.

I complete surveys for companies I care about. If they don't matter to me, I won't invest my time to give them feedback. I want to help them become better. And since I already care about them and am willing to give my time, I don't appreciate being asked to participate in a survey that disrespects me.

Whenever I contact a company, there's a reason behind it—an objective or a purpose. That implies the primary survey question. Don't ask if I was placed on hold, had to wait too long, needed to make multiple calls, or am willing to recommend them. Simply ask if they fully addressed the reason for my call.

The next item should consider if I'm happy with how they served me. Don't assume what metrics address this. Just ask if I'm pleased.

For the third and final item, provide an option for additional comments. Surveys imply a desire to hear what customers think, so I appreciate it when they provide space for me to share.

Final Thoughts

Given all this, here's the survey I'd like to take but haven't seen yet:

1. Did we resolve the reason for your call?
2. Are you pleased with how we did?
3. Do you have any other comments for us?

Thank you for asking.

SEVEN TIPS TO CONDUCT ENGAGING CUSTOMER SURVEYS

INCORPORATE BEST PRACTICES INTO YOUR CUSTOMER SURVEY PROCESS

D o you survey your customers or prospects? Should you? If you already have a survey process in place, do the results meet your needs? Should it be overhauled or even retired?

Regardless of where you are on the survey continuum, don't roll out a customer survey without first knowing if it's necessary, determining your goals, and having a well-designed plan.

Here are seven tips to conduct engaging surveys:

1. Determine Your Why

Decide what you want your customer survey to accomplish. Never do a survey until you know why you're doing it. The worst reasons to do a survey are because everyone else is or because you think you're supposed to. If it doesn't make good business sense, don't do it.

Here are some possible reasons you should have a customer survey: To improve the level of customer service, to reduce customer churn, or to close more sales.

But don't try to achieve all three objectives with one survey. Pick one.

2. Fine-Tune Your Focus

Next, you need to narrow your focus. Don't expect that one customer survey will meet the needs of every department throughout your organization. Thinking you can conduct one survey to give useful information to your service department and your sales staff and your marketing team is folly. Again, pick one.

3. Assign Responsibility

Based on your survey's *why* and *focus*, assign it to the department that will most benefit from the results. Then pick a person in that department to champion it. They may or may not be the person to design and implement the customer survey, but they do need to ensure it moves forward.

4. Design with Intention

In planning your customer survey, be intentional with its design.

In preparation, take as many surveys as you can from other companies to discover what you like and don't like.

Common survey issues are that they are either too long or too short. Other pet peeves include forcing users to explain their answers or not providing the option to leave a comment.

Posting a time estimate for the survey helps increase participation. Displaying a status bar increases the completion rate. Both are nice touches.

5. Test and Retest

With the design of the customer survey complete, it's time to test it. The survey designer should test it thoroughly before asking for more input. Next, have employees in the sponsoring department test it. Then solicit input from the rest of your company. Last, invite select customers to go through a beta version.

After each round of testing, implement any recommended changes to better support your objectives, but don't implement every suggestion. Just do the ones that make sense.

6. Roll Out Your Survey

At this point, you're ready to publish your survey. But don't blast it to every potential recipient, through all possible channels all at once. Instead, do a soft launch. This way, if there are errors or oversights—a real possibility, despite all your careful planning—you have a chance to fix them before everyone experiences the problem.

7. Iterate and Repeat

If you have a rolling survey that continues to collect data over time, periodically look at it to see if it needs tweaking, but do this only after waiting a sufficient amount of time and gathering enough data to do a thorough analysis of its strengths and weaknesses.

If your customer survey is a one-shot endeavor, look at what went well and what didn't. This can inform the next time you launch the survey because—unless you really bungled it—you'll want to do it again.

Final Thoughts

When done properly, customer surveys can provide valuable data and critical feedback to inform decision-making. To achieve the best results, apply these tips to your design and implementation process.

Happy surveying!

HOW TO COMBAT SURVEY FATIGUE

TOO MANY POORLY IMPLEMENTED SURVEYS HAVE CONDITIONED PEOPLE TO DISREGARD THEM

O rganizations of all types know the importance of receiving feedback from their stakeholders, be it their customers, clients, stockholders, prospects, users, participants, donors, volunteers, or advocates.

A stakeholder who feels heard is one who feels valued. This results in an increased affiliation with the organization and a growing connection to its mission.

One-on-one connections are the most effective way to accomplish this, whether it's in person, on the phone, or via email. Next on the effectiveness scale are group interactions, which lend themselves to physical meetings, video calls, and conference telephone calls. These all take time and have varying degrees of expense associated with them. But they are ineffective at obtaining feedback on a large scale.

Perhaps that's why online and automated phone surveys have taken off. Both are inexpensive ways to obtain valuable feedback and cement a stronger connection between the organization and the stakeholder. In addition to not costing much, surveys are also time conscious.

Their ease of implementation and low cost, however, have led to overuse and misuse. Too many are poorly designed. Too often they irritate stakeholders instead of ingratiating them.

Here are some reasons why surveys fail:

Too Often

I deal with some companies that ask me to take a survey at the end of every call. Sometimes I sigh and take the survey. Other times I sigh and don't. The data they collect may be actionable, but it's also trivial.

Too Long

Some surveys go on and on, presenting an array of questions, often asking the same thing but in different ways and various formats. These are clearly designed by people with a data focus but who lack a people focus. They gather my feedback but earn my ire in the process.

Too Short

Do one-question surveys really accomplish anything?

Too Soon

Often, I'm asked to evaluate the effectiveness of the call before I know the answer. I think the problem is resolved when my call ends, but time proves otherwise. Then I need to call again, even though on the survey I said the reason for my initial call was accomplished.

Too Limited

Sometimes I want to provide detailed information, either because I'm mad or because I have input I feel is valuable. Yet the survey has no way for me to provide it, just options to click with no place to write.

Too Frustrating

The opposite of surveys with no provision to give details are surveys that force it. For example, "Did the agent address your concern?" is followed up with the inane "How?" which requires a response in the form of an essay question. If I have nothing to say in a particular manner, don't compel me to make something up.

As a result of all these problems, people too often

respond to surveys by not responding. And that may be the most telling response of all. They have survey fatigue.

Final Thoughts

To develop improved surveys, companies must first require input from those who will take them. Just don't send them a poorly constructed survey with the intent to fix problems later. To recapture the full benefits of surveys, examine their use and their form. Then overhaul them as needed.

Design surveys that provide both actionable information and needed data. These new surveys need to engage stakeholders and show true appreciation, not merely spew trite platitudes. And they need to provide value to both parties.

STAFFING

Building upon our foundation of "Operations and Management," we now focus our attention on the subset of staffing.

Payroll is the largest expense in the call center, often comprising a majority of its budget. Given this, staffing and staffing-related issues become our first consideration.

Until we get a handle on call center staffing, the rest doesn't matter.

A POSITIVE ATTITUDE

HAVING THE IDEAL MINDSET IS KEY TO SUCCESS

While on a consulting assignment, two agents in the same inbound call center and with the same manager possessed opposite attitudes toward their work.

"This is the most interesting and exciting place I've ever worked," the first gushed. "Every call is different. I just love the variety."

Her coworker held a much different outlook. "This job is so boring," she complained. "I just do the same thing all day long."

The first enjoyed her work, seeing infinite variety within the seeming routine. Her enthusiasm was apparent, and her outlook positively affected her job and her teammates.

Yet her coworker only saw the routine, missing the subtle

and endless variations of a theme. Her demeanor was distressing, negatively impacting all who worked with her.

The issue of attitude also applies to outbound calling. Agents who see each call dialed as getting them one step closer to their goal can gladly work through those calls with purpose, to obtain their reward.

Conversely, agents who make each call attempt with resigned drudgery fail to have the ideal mindset to respond properly when they do reach someone willing to talk to them. As a result, they may miss their opportunity—and the sale. For these individuals, their career as an outbound agent will be painfully short. If only they could adapt the right attitude.

One outbound agent impressed me with her positive mindset. "I like making these calls," she enthused. "I enjoy the challenge of working toward my goal." She happily strove to reach her objective of closing a sale. She had the right mindset.

Inbound and Outbound Considerations

Inbound work is reactive. Inbound agents wait for calls to come in. When the phone rings, the callers—to varying degrees—want to talk to them. Each agent's job is to help callers, providing information they seek or completing a sale they desire.

Appreciation of the inbound agent's work is sometimes communicated. True, there are some rough calls, with the occasional caller who cannot be pleased, making personal threats or verbal attacks. But these are the exception.

Most inbound agents enjoy helping people and solving problems. They are less likely to be motivated by the rewards and monetary incentives of their outbound counterparts.

Outbound work is proactive. Outbound agents make calls —be it manually or at the pace of an automated dialer. Agents crank through calls, hoping to connect with a party willing to listen to their pitch and working toward the goal of making a sale or gathering information. Between these successes are a raft of rejections. It's toilsome work.

Most outbound agents are motivated by the financial rewards and recognition of reaching their goals. This enables them to persist in their work. These agents see each call as getting them one step closer to their objective of a sale. With intention, they work through those calls to obtain their reward.

Final Thoughts

Though agents can individually choose to adopt a positive attitude or conversely give in to a negative mindset, the call center manager can promote positivity to the entire staff. They can also do the opposite.

THE ART OF FINDING A CALL CENTER MANAGER
THERE ARE ONLY TWO OPTIONS TO FIND AN OPERATIONS MANAGER

"I need to find a good manager."

This statement is simple and its occurrence, common. I've heard it many times over the years, including when I worked in call centers, when I consulted for call centers, and now that I write about call centers. Despite the straightforward nature of this basic need, its successful culmination is anything but easy.

Quite simply, if you make the wrong selection, the future of your operation is in jeopardy. It only takes a few months of bad management to undo years of work spent building a smoothly functioning machine.

The problem is that the downward spiral is seldom recognized until after the damage is done. By then, good employees have left, remaining staff is demoralized, long-time customers are gone, and callers are fuming. Despite the careful vetting process, employment screens, interviews, background checks, and personal references, your hand-picked manager—the hero you thought would solve all your problems and make your job easier—failed to meet expectations.

Once again, you're pressed into finding a good manager.

The options before you are deceptively simple. There are but two. You can promote from within or hire from without.

Promote from Within

When you promote existing call center employees into management, several items work in your favor.

First, you know them and their work ethic.

Next, they have already proven themselves, perhaps as a shift supervisor, a trainer, a lead agent, or maybe all three.

Third, they know your business. They will not need to be trained in how your organization operates.

Last, they know the industry. They *get* call center work and understand the toils of being an agent.

The downside is they seldom have management experience. This means they need management training, followed by close supervision as they grow into their job. This doesn't happen quickly. Along the way, they'll make mistakes. The hope is that the mistakes will be minor and the successes will greatly outweigh the errors.

Hire from Without

The other approach is to hire an experienced manager. This solves all the issues surrounding management training. Yes, the new manager will still require some oversight in the beginning, but the time frame should be much shorter than for someone with no managerial experience.

The disadvantages of hiring from the outside, however, are numerous.

First, you have no work history together, and you don't know their character.

Next, they will need to prove themselves to you, which takes time and may not happen.

Third, they don't know your business or operation.

Last, they may lack call center experience. And if they have it, you may be faced with needing to retrain them to fit your operation.

Final Thoughts

There is no easy approach when hiring a good manager for your call center. There is a real art to it, but that's what makes this industry fun. After all, if anyone could do it, then everyone would.

Look at your past and present call center leadership staff. Were most promoted from within or hired from the outside? Use the answer to inform your next step.

BE NICE

WHAT MAY SEEM COMMON SENSE TO US MAY NOT BE TO YOUR FRONTLINE STAFF

A friend works for a company that helps government agencies provide better service to its customers. One division works with call centers, and another addresses walk-in traffic. That's where my friend works.

Often his company needs to address the basics. Sometimes they must start with a simple instruction that seems common sense: "Be nice to the people you serve."

Inevitably someone asks, "Why?"

So the second step becomes explaining the reasons behind the need to be nice.

While it's laughable that anyone needs to teach this seemingly self-evident idea to a service sector employee, apparently not everyone understands it. These staffers need to first learn this lesson, then master the concept, and finally apply it to the people they serve.

In a practical sense, *be nice* stands as an astute guiding principle. After all, if our call center agents are nice to callers, doesn't that direct the bulk of their actions?

And yet, I can't imagine day one of agent training opening with a lesson titled "Be Nice." The ability to be nice should stand as a requirement for hire, a trait we screen for in the interview process. But if one person slips through who isn't nice, then, short of termination, *Be Nice* training is in order.

Perhaps an entire shift—or even the whole call center—has degraded into a staff of not-nice employees. Instruction on how to be nice is required to overhaul the shift or remake the center.

What would *Be Nice* training entail?

Again, it seems self-evident, but here are the high points:

Follow the Golden Rule

"Do unto others as you would have them do unto you" stands as the guiding principle for *Be Nice*. When we treat others as we wish to be treated, we take a huge first step toward being nice.

Smile

Though no one can see a smile on a telephone call, people can hear it. We should smile often at the people we talk to on the phone. If it helps, have a mirror at your station to remind you. Personally, I find a mirror disconcerting, yet as I use video tools to talk with people—which allows me to see myself as others see me—I'm reminded of the importance of smiling when I talk.

Be Friendly

Don't be surly. We've all encountered surliness in customer service situations, both in person and over the phone. Surly repels; friendly attracts. Remember, it's much easier to be friendly when we smile, while surly is more likely when we frown.

Respond Fast

Part of being nice is being responsive. It's frustrating to have to wait to have our question answered or pay our bill while an employee completes a trivial conversation with a coworker or wraps up a personal phone call. Yet this happens all the time.

We notice it when we're in person, but over the phone we can't see unresponsiveness. Agent indifference toward callers, however, results in us enduring more rings or listening longer to on-hold music.

Solve Problems

The main reason for customer service is to resolve customer issues, so the goal of *Be Nice* training is to solve problems. This includes resolving the issue and callers agreeing that we did.

This is where first call resolution (FCR) comes in, which most of the time promotes effective problem resolution. Too often, however, call centers focus on average call time, which effectively encourages agents to offer simplistic answers, refer callers to someone else, or transfer the caller. This doesn't solve problems, and it isn't nice. But it does keep the average call time low.

Final Thoughts

Be nice at work and be nice at home. Be nice to others, and they'll often be nice to you in return. Be nice in all you do, and you'll make an impact everywhere you go.

BE CAREFUL WHAT YOU SAY

PEOPLE JUDGE THE COMPANY WE REPRESENT ON EVERY SINGLE PHONE CALL

I once had a call center agent who offered commentary at the end of every call. Her comments ranged from snarky to crass. Occasionally she voiced her opinion a bit too quickly—before the caller had hung up or while the voice logger was still recording. In addition, her unfiltered diatribe irritated her coworkers in adjacent cubicles. Eventually we reigned in her problematic habit, but I don't think we stopped it altogether.

A Need to Vent

I get that sometimes we need to vent. But this should be rare, not common. And, most certainly, the caller should never be privy to our opinions, such as this agent's thoughts about a caller's intellectual abilities or education.

Occasionally agents need to go out of rotation for a moment to gather their thoughts and recalibrate their focus before they dive into the next call. On the rarest of occasions, an agent may require an unscheduled break.

If you work in a call center, you know that this post-call commentary happens. You may even do it yourself, perhaps in your mind or maybe under your breath, but it shouldn't happen aloud. That's simply unprofessional—doubly so if the caller hears even a fragment of it.

Recently I experienced the other end of this. I had called a company, and afterward I heard the agent's commentary—about me. As we said our goodbyes, but before I could hang up, she sighed and whispered, "What a nice man."

My mind went spinning. First was the shock that she spoke before disconnecting our call. Next was that I experienced the caller's side of hearing an agent's post-call opinion. And third was that I had done nothing special to earn the positive label she gave me. Though I deserved no credit, I hoped the rest of her day was a bit better because of our interaction.

In all my years in the call center industry, I can't remember an agent making a positive statement after a call. Either it's negative, or it's nonexistent.

Callers Talk About Agents Too

What agents may not realize is that callers do this same thing when it comes to agents. Here are some things I've thought or said after a call:

"I don't think they have a clue."

"What they said made absolutely no sense."

"I have no expectation they'll follow through."

"Maybe I should call again and talk to a rep who actually knows what's going on."

When I—and every other caller—make these statements, they might be addressing the agent, but they're not really about the agent. They're about the company the agent represents.

Every Call Matters

That's why every call matters. Each call is an opportunity to impress the caller and draw them into your company. Alternately, every call has the potential to drive them away. Unfortunately, one poor call can negate several good ones.

Over the years I've experienced both great calls and bad. I often share these examples so we can learn from them and do better. One call stands out as the best of the best. It was a help desk call that lasted over an hour. As the rep worked to resolve my software issue, she kept up a rapport-building conversation.

Most help desk agents politely place callers on hold

while waiting for various tasks to complete. This one didn't. She maintained an engaging dialogue with me—though I mostly listened, and she mostly talked. She told me how much she liked her job and what a great company she worked for. We talked a bit about the general area where she lived and the climate—a perfect fit for her. She also shared other tidbits that were neither too personal nor uninteresting. Throughout it all she exuded positivity, and her infectious demeanor rubbed off on me.

The call ended, but the memory of it remains. Now, many months later, I'm dismayed to admit I no longer remember her name. But I do remember the company she worked for.

That's a lesson for us all.

Final Thoughts

What are you doing to provide lasting memories with your staff and customers? Have you empowered your staff to make lasting memories with their callers?

DON'T MAKE EXTRA WORK FOR YOUR AGENTS

RECOVER FROM YOUR MISTAKES AND DON'T COMPOUND THEM

O nce I received an email from a company saying that I could download my statement. When I went to retrieve the document, however, it wasn't available. The past twenty-four statements were, but not the one their email said was waiting for me.

Since I usually access this information through their app, I went to their website and attempted to log in. I was unsuccessful. The password I used last time (which was likely more than a year before) didn't work. I needed to go through the I-forgot-my-password routine. After waiting too long to receive the temporary password, I successfully logged in. To my dismay, the sought-after document wasn't there either.

At the bottom of the page was a link to email them with questions. Having invested half an hour at this point and being no closer to viewing my statement, I was frustrated. I concisely shared the situation and clicked *send*.

To my surprise, I received a response within minutes. The agent wrote that someone sent the email notice prematurely. "The problem has been corrected and your statement is now available for download."

Excited by the progress, I returned to the app to access my statement, but the document was still not available. Then I tried their website—again. It wasn't there either. This time I spotted a toll-free number for customer support.

I dialed the number. The recording said to expect an eighteen-minute wait. I selected the option to receive a call-back when it was my turn. Eleven minutes later, the phone rang. Elated, I expected to talk to a rep, but instead I heard a recording, followed by music on hold. I waited the full eighteen minutes after all.

When the agent eventually answered, I explained the situation, making little effort to hide my frustration.

After doing some checking and consulting with a coworker, the agent confirmed the initial email went out in error, the rep who handled my follow-up email gave me incorrect information, and my statement still wasn't online.

"When will it be available?"

"I don't know, but legally we have six more days before it has to be posted," came the snarky reply. "Just keep checking."

Fuming, I checked periodically throughout the day. On the fourth try, my statement was available. I'd invested about an hour in total to accomplish what should have been a simple task.

Along the way, they sent me a brief customer service survey. My concise comment was, "Don't email me to download my statement before it's actually available."

I'm still waiting for a response.

In summary, this company sent an email in error, which resulted in me contacting their customer support center and causing them to perform one needless activity. To compound the situation, the rep who answered my email mishandled it by providing me with more wrong information. My subsequent call to them was a second needless activity. Sending me a customer service survey served as a third needless activity. Assuming someone looks at my survey response, this will cause a fourth needless activity—all because of one errant email.

I doubt I was the only customer to get the email prematurely. How many others also received it? Thousands? Tens of thousands? More? If only 1 percent complained to the contact center, how many more needless activities took place?

I'm sure the contact center agents had a stressful day. It all could have been avoided if their company hadn't sent a mass email message too soon. Sometimes we can be our own worst enemies—and the contact center often pays for it.

Final Thoughts

All people and all companies make mistakes from time to time. Though you can't undo the error, you can control how you respond. Do you compound the problem or resolve it on the first try?

Then, once the crisis has passed, consider what to do to make sure the original blunder doesn't happen again. (In the case of the company in question, it happened two more times.)

WORK-AT-HOME OPPORTUNITIES
THE BENEFITS OF HOME-BASED TELEPHONE AGENTS

In the past few years, we've seen an unprecedented move to pursue work-at-home opportunities in call centers. Granted, some operations were already there. But others outright reject home-based staff as an option. Still, most companies embrace a distributed workforce as a new way of doing business—even if they're not there yet. And many operations have moved in that direction, albeit with varying degrees of interest and success.

Work-at-home opportunities apply to all employees, both agents and non-agents. At the risk of reviewing what you already know, here are some reasons you should consider tapping home-based employees.

Retain Existing Staff

Providing employees with the option to work from home may mean the difference between keeping a great employee and losing them to another company—even a competitor—who offers that option.

Sometimes an employee's situation changes, and they can't—or no longer feel comfortable—coming into your office to work. But you can keep them as an employee if you offer them work-at-home opportunities.

Attract New Staff

When you hire employees, having work-at-home opportunities for them to consider may mean the difference between you hiring a new team member and losing a great prospect. Don't miss out on an otherwise-qualified candidate because you don't allow for them to work from home once they've proven themselves.

Expand Your Labor Market

Most every call center struggles to find qualified employees. Though most prefer to pursue hiring from the labor market where the call center is located, this limits prospects. By offering work-at-home opportunities, you can expand your labor pool to cover anyone, in any area, who has stable internet service.

New Agent Solutions

There are also a couple of new work-at-home opportunities that present themselves once you remove the restrictions of working from a centralized office. Though these aren't impossible outcomes to realize with your in-house staff, they're much more realistic to achieve from a home-based workforce. These are split shifts and on-demand work.

Split Shifts: Split shifts occur when an employee doesn't work in one continuous block of time, but in two or even three smaller blocks. This can be ideal in meeting scheduling forecasts.

This depends on the specific needs of your call center and what your traffic looks like, but it could include working at the beginning of the business day and again toward the end. Or it may be taking calls for a few hours in the midmorning and a few more hours midafternoon.

It's a lot to expect someone to travel to a call center to only work a few hours, leave, and then come back for a few more. But it's much more realistic when someone's already at home, can quickly log in, work, and then log out.

On-Demand Work: Split shifts also point to another solution, which is on-demand work. This is effectively having someone on standby for when your call center gets busy. If they're already at home and have a flexible schedule, they may be more than willing to log in and take calls to handle an unexpected traffic burst and log out when things return to normal.

Just make sure to treat your on-demand employees fairly. In exchange for their flexibility, pay them more for on-demand work. It also means only contacting them when you really need them and promising them a minimum amount of pay when you do, such as for at least one hour. What you want to avoid is having someone take calls for only a few minutes at a time, multiple times throughout the day. This will lead to frustrated staff and burnout.

Final Thoughts

Work-at-home opportunities abound. Be sure to make the most of them to best staff your call center, maintain a qualified workforce, and serve your callers.

THE BENEFITS OF HOME-BASED CALL CENTER AGENTS

DISCOVER WHY EVERY CALL CENTER SHOULD MOVE TOWARD HAVING A REMOTE STAFF

M any businesses struggle to find entry-level employees. This includes the call center industry. Though the technology to allow for remote work has existed for a long time—and continues to improve—some call centers are reluctant to embrace the option of home-based call center agents.

This may be due to several factors.

A key one is the challenge of managing a distributed workforce.

Another is being able to ensure quality.

Third is a tendency to want to continue doing what we've always done and are comfortable doing.

Yet business dynamics continue to change. And the rate of change continues to accelerate. If your call center continues to pursue a paradigm of having all employees work from a centralized location, now is the time to challenge that perception and reconfigure your operation to address today's needs and prepare for tomorrow's opportunities.

Here are some of the key benefits of hiring home-based call center agents.

Tap Homebound Workers

Some otherwise-qualified employees want to work but for varying reasons are homebound. This may be due to preference or circumstances, but the fact remains that they are eager candidates. It's just that they can't go to work, so you need to bring the work to them. Fortunately, this is easy to do—as well as being a perfect fit—for call center work.

Though some situations aren't suitable, such as people tasked with childcare or eldercare, other contexts are a nonissue. This includes people who lack transportation, live too far from your office, have mobility issues, or struggle with social anxieties. These people can potentially work remotely and function as ideal home-based call center agents.

Expanded Labor Pool

If your local labor market lacks qualified or willing candidates, has unrealistic compensation expectations, or suffers from a low unemployment rate, explore an untapped or under-reached remote labor market to find home-based call center agents to staff your operation and fill your roster.

Flexible Scheduling

As we mentioned in the chapter "Work-At-Home Opportunities," many call centers could benefit by scheduling people for split shifts, working an hour or two at various times throughout the day to meet traffic peaks. In addition is the dream of having on-demand workers who could log in to process calls to deal with an unexpected deluge of traffic, be it for a few minutes or several hours.

Both these options become realistic with home-based call center agents. Many are willing to accept odd schedules or be available for on-demand work. They measure their commute in steps, not miles or minutes. And, unless your operation uses videoconferencing, their appearance doesn't matter. They don't need to follow an office-based dress code. Since they're working from home, they can log in within seconds and take calls for short shifts or on-demand, as well as regular shifts.

Of course, not every home-based employee will embrace this paradigm, but some will, and they may even prefer it.

Save on Facility Costs

With home-based call center agents, you have fewer people working in your office. This means you can scale back on your facility.

Taken to its logical conclusion, you will have no staff working onsite. As a result, you'll be able to close your office, rent out the space, or sell your building. This will cut your costs and bolster your profits.

Provide Safe Employment

Though this concern is not as high as it once was, we should prepare for the possibility that a pandemic could one day reemerge, perhaps as an even more dangerous threat. In this scenario, working from home removes employees from the physical contact of others, eliminating the possibility of getting a virus from their coworkers or giving one to them.

Final Thoughts

Consider all these benefits of home-based call center agents. What do you need to do to embrace them more fully?

WORK-AT-HOME FOR EVERYONE

A HOME-BASED OFFICE FOR NON-AGENT STAFF

For the past couple of decades—since 2000, long before it was a trend—I've worked from an office in my home.

The benefits of working at home are many: no commute time or travel expense, no dress code, no need to pack a lunch or go out to eat (another money saver), and no coworkers dropping by to chat when I need to focus.

Working at home enables me to accomplish much in a shorter time. I relish it.

Working at home also presents some challenges: distractions abound, no one's present to hold you accountable, food is readily available when a craving hits, and if you want to take a nap—you can. I've even heard of some skipping their shower and working in their pajamas.

Another issue is that it's impossible to leave work and go home, since you're already there.

A Need for Self-Control and Boundaries

Successfully working at home requires discipline. You need self-control to work when you're supposed to (and to not work when you're not supposed to), to approach each day with the same degree of professionalism you would in an office environment, and to say "no" to every distraction.

For me, as a solopreneur, I pay a price if my focus waivers. The work must still be done, and I'm the one who must do it.

When our children were younger, I set a firm rule: Between 9:00 a.m. and 5:00 p.m., Daddy's working, so don't go into his office. At times, they would stand mute just outside my door, looking pathetic.

So I amended my decree. Between 9:00 a.m. and 5:00 p.m., don't let Daddy *see* you.

That didn't work either.

"I know you're out there. I can hear you breathing." Eventually we arrived at a workable arrangement, but they did watch the time. They'd often bound into my office at exactly 5:00 p.m. Their mother, however, claimed immunity to my expectations. We never did resolve that.

After a while, I made one adjustment. I'd take an afternoon break to coincide with our kids' homecoming from school. They'd share their day with me, often with excitement, sometimes in despair. Eight hours of highlights spewed forth in a matter of seconds. Then they'd finish and head off to do their own thing, and I'd return to work. By the time their mother came home, the school day's headlines were long forgotten. They'd say hello but little more. She'd ask how their day was or what had happened, and they'd just shrug.

The Right Environment

For the first decade I worked in the basement, and my office had no windows. Many a time, I'd break for lunch or dinner, surprised to see how the weather had changed.

Now my office resides in a vacated bedroom, complete with a view. This vista sometimes becomes a distraction. Once I watched four bunnies frolicking in my backyard— and then took time to write a blog post celebrating their exuberance. Another time, while on the phone, my caller asked if she heard birds in the background. My window was open. Who would have guessed? I'd tuned out their happy songs, but my headset's microphone did not.

Final Thoughts

While some can work at home, others should not. Considerations include worker motivation and their degree of self-discipline, the home office environment, the presence of family, and the technological infrastructure.

If the employee is a match, decide if the requirements of their job are a good fit for working from home. If it's a go, consider what support you can offer them as far as dealing with technical issues and crafting a balance between work and home—since they work where they live.

In my case, I'm an ideal candidate. I get more done in less time. I'm happier and enjoy a better work-life balance.

MANAGING A DISTRIBUTED WORKFORCE
THE CALL CENTER BECOMES THE CONTACT DEPARTMENT

T he label *call center* amuses me. In short, a call center is neither exclusively calls nor centralized.

First, most call centers now process more than just calls, such as emails and text chats. Second is that call centers are increasingly decentralized, even though a decentralized center is an oxymoron.

The decentralization of the call center first occurred by linking multiple centers together and more recently by extending the operation to encompass home-based agents. As a result, the call center workforce is geographically distributed.

When I was last involved in the day-to-day operations of a call center, I worked on interconnecting disparate locations together to share technologies, gain greater economies-of-scale, and blend staffs and call queues.

At that time, the nascent work-at-home model was hampered by technical limitations, so my focus was on distributing calls to other centers, not to individual homes. But technology has changed that.

Here are some tips to guide you in effectively managing a decentralized workforce.

Have a Clear Policy

Don't decide on the suitability of home-based agents on a case-by-case basis, which too often happens. Either you allow working at home, or you don't. Make a firm policy and stick with it. Don't subject employees to uncertainty or inconsistency.

Have the Right Managers

The default management style of many is "management by walking around." This approach—though often effective in a one-location operation—no longer works in a distributed environment. As such, true management skills must be implemented to oversee all staff in all locations.

If you want to have a distributed workforce and your manager can't handle it, either provide the needed training or find a new manager. Don't summarily tell those who can or are successfully working at home that the right to do so has been rescinded.

Avoid Us Versus Them

A multilocation office often produces an *us-versus-them* mentality. Everyone at your location is *us*, and all other employees become *them*. In truth, everyone in the company or call center should be *us*, regardless of location. Otherwise, remote staff becomes *them* at the main office, disregarding them in the process.

Imagine receiving an email that there are donuts in the break room, only to discover that the break room referenced is not down the hall but sixty miles away. Also ensure that the same rules and expectations apply to all employees, regardless of location.

Final Thoughts

With these concepts in mind, form a plan to move forward. Communicate that plan. Then follow it.

Deviate from it only when there is a good reason to do so, and then only after getting input from the entire workforce at all locations.

CUSTOMER SERVICE

With appropriate staffing in place, we now turn our attention to customer service. Serving customers and prospects is the reason that call centers exist.

Therefore, we must give customer service the proper attention it deserves. If we fail to serve our customers, our call center fails to fulfill its mission, and we put our jobs and the company's future in jeopardy.

As you work to build up your call center staff, make customer service a priority.

SERVICE SOLD IT

DOES THE SERVICE YOU PROVIDE DRAW BUSINESS IN OR PUSH IT AWAY?

G rowing up, I remember a radio commercial with the tagline, "Service sold it." Even as a young child, I understood that this company provided such a high level of service that their reputation was sufficient for them to gain new business.

Over the years, I've heard this mantra repeated, either verbatim or conceptually, by various local, national, and international companies. Yet I no longer give this grandiose platitude serious consideration. These words now have a hollow ring to them. They reek of disingenuous assurance and hold an empty promise.

What was once good business turned into nothing more than good ad copy, which is now simply lost in the clutter of messages we no longer believe. In fact, the louder businesses trumpet this claim, the less I trust it. The greater the hype, the more I assume their service is lousy and their ad campaign's only goal is to convince us—and them—of the contrary. To paraphrase George Bernard Shaw, "He who can, does. He who cannot, talks about it."

It seems no one provides good service anymore.

In contrasting my experiences of customer service success with failures, I realize that being local and being small are two elements that decidedly allow the potential for better customer service. These, however, are not requirements. The real key is relationship.

With each unfavorable example I considered, I dealt with a department, not an individual—not really. The representative had no accountability to me and no stake in the outcome. With subsequent calls, I would talk to a different person. To them I was not a customer as much as an annoyance. I had no real value to them. I was just another phone call—a problem—to get rid of in the shortest time possible. Then they could go on to the next call and eventually punch out for the day.

Yet, with each company I cite as a positive example, my primary contact was a specific person who made the difference. This was someone who genuinely cared about my situation and had a real interest in the outcome. It was someone willing to put in extra time to make me his or her most important priority, to do what was required.

While these things are critical and most appreciated, an underlying theme is that in each case we established a rapport and developed a connection first. Because of our one-to-one personal relationship, exceptional customer service could flow from it with ease.

Final Thoughts

Does your in-house call center provide this same one-to-one connection with your customers? What about outsource call centers to your clients' callers?

Can you honestly say, believe, and prove that *service sold it*? If not, what changes do you need to make?

FIVE TIPS FOR AGENT CUSTOMER SERVICE SUCCESS

MASTER THE ART OF EFFECTIVE CALL CENTER COMMUNICATION

S ome people think working in a call center is easy because they like to talk. But that doesn't guarantee agent customer service success. Instead, successful agents need to work at it. Yes, this is easier for some than others, but no one is born with the ability to serve customers with excellence.

Here are five tips to pursue to develop agent customer service success.

1. Develop Active Listening Skills

Better customer interaction begins with active listening. This starts by removing distractions and giving your whole self to listening. Don't just focus on the words they say, but also on how they voice them, as well as what they might not be telling you.

Then address their concerns—both those stated and those implied.

2. Tap Nonverbal Communication

Communication has three components: the words said, the tone of voice, and body language. Most communication occurs through body language, which doesn't come across over the phone—unless it's a video call.

That leaves words and tone. In addition to their words, key in on the tone of voice as well, which carries more communication information than the actual words spoken.

To build rapport and empathy requires understanding the emotions and needs of customers. This means going beyond what they say. Doing so helps provide a more personalized and satisfactory customer experience.

3. Employ Effective Communication Techniques

Agents should use appropriate language, tone, and nonverbal cues to convey messages clearly and profession-ally. Yes, your body language comes through over the phone. People can hear you smile. They can also hear you frown. Both impact the way your words come across and how customers receive your message.

Also avoid industry jargon and insider shorthand. Use simple language that customers can understand with ease.

4. Aim to Solve Problems and Resolve Conflicts

Equip yourself with problem-solving skills to handle customer concerns efficiently. This means addressing fully the reason for their call. Don't just do the minimum and assume it's good enough. Each call should end with the customer having full confidence that you addressed their issue—or that you will. There should be no need for them to call you back.

Sometimes, however, before you can tackle their concern, you'll first need to address conflict.

To master both problem-solving and conflict resolution, take classes, go to seminars, and read books to learn how to better deal with difficult or irate customers, resolve conflicts, and de-escalate tense situations. This brings us to the fifth tip of agent customer service success.

5. Embrace Continuous Training and Feedback

Agent success is not something you learn once. Instead, it's something you continue to learn. Be open to regular training sessions to hone your proficiency. Embrace feedback to improve your communication skills. This includes learning from your mistakes and receiving constructive feedback from trainers and coaches.

Final Thoughts

Follow these agent customer service success tips to help you enhance your customer service effectiveness.

START GREAT CUSTOMER EXPERIENCE WITH CUSTOMER SERVICE ESSENTIALS

TO DELIGHT CUSTOMERS, START WITH THE BASICS AND BUILD ON THAT FOUNDATION

I n the call center space, customer experience looms as the current buzzword. But beyond all the talk, I wonder if it's not just a new label on a theme that's been around for a long time. The basis for customer experience resides in customer service.

Customer service is the reason call centers exist in the first place and functions as the distinguishing factor between excellence and failure. Here are some customer service elements all call centers should pursue to provide a great customer experience.

Timely Reactions

First on the list is the imperative to not waste the caller's time. This means answering calls quickly, with minimal hold time, no transfers, and a quick resolution. Too many callers brace themselves for a long ordeal each time they phone a call center. This is the wrong message to send. Yet their experiences support this conclusion.

Yes, you need to match optimum scheduling with a desire for speed, but strive to strike an agreeable balance. Having the right number of agents available to meet projected call forecasts and adjusting to unexpected traffic spikes is key.

Efficient Interactions

Callers also want their communication with your call center to be proficient. They object to giving their account number again when they've already entered it. They also bristle at the need to repeat information each time their call is transferred. And if they must be placed on hold for the agent to check something, they will usually understand, but try to keep the hold time short and restrict the number of holds to a minimum.

Just as you want your agents to be efficient on every call, callers also expect you to be efficient with their time. Respect them and honor the investment they made in calling you.

Positive Responses

Tell callers what you can do for them, not what you can't. Learn positive phrases and interject them into conversations whenever possible. Talk with a smile on your face, and callers will hear it in your words. Keep an upbeat attitude, even when dealing with difficult situations.

Accurate Results

Most of all, callers expect the information you provide to be correct. Too many callers have talked to agents who will say anything, whether it's right or not, just to end the call. Callers want to trust the information you give them. They also expect you to follow through and do what you promise.

They want results they can depend on.

Memorable Outcomes

Beyond the length of the call, callers want to feel good about what occurred, both when they hang up and in the days and weeks that follow. Often it takes time for the veracity of a call to become known. Customers may not realize until it's too late that they received wrong information or that the steps the agent took didn't solve the problem. Then they must call a second time, and they won't be happy about it. You want to avoid this.

Instead, make each outcome memorable and eliminate the need for follow-up calls.

Final Thoughts

When call centers offer these customer-service essentials, they're on their way to delivering a great customer experience to their callers. That's what customer service is all about.

Though you can spend a lot of time fixated on providing great customer experiences—or whatever the current industry buzzword is—the reality is that this hot-topic-of-the-day usually goes back to customer service essentials.

Start with a focus on customer service and build upon it.

DON'T FORGET THE HUMAN TOUCH
TECHNOLOGY MAY SAVE MONEY, BUT HUMAN AGENTS MAKE THE DIFFERENCE

We hear a lot about artificial intelligence (AI), and we're going to hear a lot more about it. Some claim AI is the future of the call center industry, saving money and retaining customers. Others fear it's the end of customer service as we know it. Neither is right; nor are they both wrong.

But AI isn't the only technology in our call centers. We have digital assistants to help our agents and automated bots to help our customers. Before that, we had interactive voice response (IVR) and auto-attendant solutions.

Regardless of the technology or the era it comes from, each innovation brings with it the promise to speed resolutions and reduce labor expenses. To some degree, past technologies accomplished this. Yet each also fell short of meeting expectations.

In most cases, however, the implementation of technology has brought with it the corresponding ire of the customers it's supposed to help.

In some cases, technology—especially AI—can make a real mess of things. When this happens, human intervention is the only way to correct the problem. This assumes, of course, that people are available to intercede and fix technology's error.

Here are some things human agents can do that technology can't do or can't do well.

Correct Miscommunication

Technology struggles to correct its mistakes. When it determines what path to take, it persists on that course even if it's the wrong one. Often, miscommunication devolves into such a quagmire that the simplest approach—sometimes the only one—is to terminate communication and start over.

This is an ideal time for human intervention to clarify the customer's concern and redirect action toward the right solution. This means that human agents need to have the ability to override technology. They also need to have both the training and confidence to know when to do so.

Calm Frustrated Customers

Technology struggles to know when customers are upset, and it fails to respond in a truly comforting way. Yes, through algorithms AI can detect anger or frustration and attempt to react. Yet customers are apt to discern any attempt of AI to diffuse their concerns as disingenuous. This will escalate their tension, not defuse it.

A successful outcome requires a real person, someone who will listen, comprehend, and sympathize. Though no human agent can accomplish this all the time, their chance of success is much higher than that of a machine.

Respond to Complex Issues

Convoluted problems can escape the ability of AI to comprehend and successfully navigate. This is especially true when a situation is unique, something AI has not yet encountered. Human ingenuity shines in these situations.

Offer Empathy

Sometimes customers feel a need to vent. Ironically, this is often over the failure of technological solutions to address their concern. Though AI can determine the need to give an apology and mimic the right words to say, can it do so with empathy? Will the response come across as sincere? Will the customer feel heard?

A person has a much better chance of doing this successfully than a computer.

Final Thoughts

Don't forget to offer the personal touch of a human agent to best serve customers whenever needed.

Though AI technology will continue to improve, causing fewer problems and producing more satisfying solutions, don't plan on replacing your staff. Though you will not need as many agents, you will need some. And the skill set of these super agents will carry higher requirements than current ones.

Being able to offer the human touch will distinguish contact centers from their technology-only counterparts. In an era when technology surrounds us and threatens to overwhelm, a human customer service agent stands as a core distinction between offering solutions that are close versus ones that are comprehensive and complete.

AMAZE YOUR CUSTOMERS . . . OR ANNOY THEM

EACH CUSTOMER-FACING INTERACTION HAS TWO POSSIBLE OUTCOMES

I nforming callers of the expected time before an agent will be available is an appreciated gesture. Usually the estimate is reliable, and often the agent answers sooner—but not always.

My worst experience was being told I was "next in line," a promise that repeated every fifteen seconds. After thirty minutes, I placed the call on hold and left for dinner, curious to see what would happen. I returned to hear the same announcement and waited another two hours. I put the call on hold again and went to bed. The next morning, after a total hold time of fourteen hours, I was still "next in line."

I placed a second simultaneous call, which was also "next in line." I disconnected both calls and redialed. I was still "next in line." After waiting another two hours of being "next in line," someone responded to one of my many email pleas for help.

It was the president of the company, and he was not pleased to hear about my ordeal.

Schedule a Callback

Having the choice to be called back instead of waiting on hold is a nice option, provided the company follows through as requested. I don't normally do this because the callback often interrupts something more important.

Usually, the callback works as promised. But sometimes no one ever calls. Once I received a callback but on a different number and on a different day than I had requested.

Interactive Voice Response

IVR would be great if it actually sped up my call, but I have doubts. Once I made repeated tech support calls to a company, each time navigating through seven levels of prompts, taking almost two minutes per call if I listened to the full recordings. But the person who would eventually answer could never help me and would transfer me to someone else.

Worse are endless IVR loops, forcing me to hang up when I get stuck.

In addition, pressing zero for an agent should always be an option, but many times it isn't.

Re-entering Information

Often I must enter information—such as an account number or phone number—before being connected to a person, but then the agent makes me repeat it. This is exasperating and poor customer service.

I expect call centers to know my number and display it to agents, but this commonsense feature is too often lacking. Don't ask a caller to tell you what you should already know.

Final Thoughts

Does your call center technology amaze or annoy customers?

HOW WOULD YOU LIKE US TO CONTACT YOU?

WHEN YOU ASK A PROSPECT WHICH COMMUNICATION CHANNEL THEY PREFER, BE SURE TO HONOR IT

After our basement flooded and the insurance company said, "Sorry, you're not covered," I knew it was time to find a new insurer. As I scanned a website for a local insurance agent's phone number, I spotted an information request form. I completed it, including the customer-centric option: "How should we contact you?"

The five choices were phone, email, text, fax, and mail. While the last three didn't appeal to me, I vacillated between a phone call and an email. I selected email, largely because it would provide a written record of our communication.

I clicked submit.

Soon my phone rang. It was an agent from my prospective insurance company. Normally a phone call would have been fine, even preferable. But why did they ask what I wanted if they weren't going to honor my request? We weren't off to a good start.

I reminded the agent that I preferred email communication, and we switched to email for our subsequent interactions. To the company's credit, the agent stuck with that channel. As we moved toward finalizing the policy, I had a series of questions more suited to the efficiency of a phone call. This caught the agent off guard, but she answered my questions and confirmed my understanding. I now have insurance through her company.

This reminds me of the time I looked for a new auto mechanic. The one I picked allowed people to request an appointment online. I filled out the form. They, too, asked how I wanted to be contacted. I selected "text" since I assumed this was the ideal channel for a succinct confirmation message.

They emailed me.

The date I requested was full, and so was my second choice. Obviously, their appointment module was a static form and not integrated with their actual schedule. I emailed them back with a third date, and I received a follow up email with a question. We went back and forth with email messages, taking most of the day to set an appointment. A phone call would have been so much more efficient.

I soon realized that email was their default mode. Though I've requested texts to confirm appointments, they've never once done so. It's always email. When I ask them to call me when my car is ready, they usually don't communicate at all. The only time they did call me was when they under-billed me. Apparently, they thought a phone call was the best way to resolve that.

Considering this, a few thoughts come to mind.

Offering Options Is Good

Letting prospects and customers pick how they prefer to be contacted is a customer-friendly move and a great idea, especially given that people usually have choices of who to do business with and are quick to exercise those choices.

Not Honoring Those Options Is Bad

Not using the channel a customer requests is worse than not offering the option in the first place. If you can't—or won't—contact customers by the method they request, don't bother to ask.

Not Responding Is Worse

Making no effort to contact customers when they request it is the worst possible mistake. How hard would it be for the customer service rep for my mechanic to let me know my car is ready? She can call, email, or text. Instead, I'm left to guess when I can pick up my car—or even if it's done.

Know When to Switch Channels

Sometimes a preferred channel bogs down communication. When emails or texts go back and forth without resolution, it's time to pick up the phone, but before doing so, make that suggestion through the customer's channel of choice.

Final Thoughts

Asking how prospects want you to contact them is great if you follow through, but if you don't do as they request, it's better to not offer the option.

Also, know when it's appropriate to switch channels. Providing excellent customer service relies on excellent communication, whether it's within the requested channel or on another one.

HOW TO ENHANCE THE CUSTOMER EXPERIENCE

PURSUE BIG-PICTURE SOLUTIONS, NOT INCREMENTAL IMPROVEMENTS

There's a lot of talk about customer experience and ways to enhance it. Though this is the right outcome, too often the approach to get there is shortsighted. Making incremental changes to improve one metric may help a bit, but how many metrics must you improve and by how much for the customer to realize an enhanced experience? And how much stress will your frontline staff endure to get there?

Instead of focusing on the minutiae of data that call center systems are so good at producing, step back and address big-picture issues. These will have the greatest impact on improving customer experience. And the side effect of these changes will make it easier, not harder, for your staff to do their job with excellence.

Integrate Isolated Databases

How many places do you store customer data and the information your staff needs to serve callers? How easy is it for agents to get all relevant information displayed on a single monitor—or even two?

Ideally you want everything in one place, in a unified database. Sometimes, however, this isn't feasible. In those instances, it's critical to be able to move seamlessly from one to the other. Consider how often customer service representatives give wrong information simply because they aren't looking in the right place.

Integrating or interconnecting databases for seamless customer experience is something for vendors to accomplish. It's usually too complex for end users to solve. Therefore, investigate whether the software you're considering will hamper your team from fully using the tools you already have. Sometimes the solution is there, but you can't tap into its power because of how you deployed it.

Remove Internal Silos of Control

Many companies operate as a group of disengaged fiefdoms. This occurs in departments such as operations, marketing, sales, accounting, tech support, and so forth. When management measures each department head for that unit's individual performance—disconnected from the company's overall objectives—the result is managers doing what is in the best interest of themselves, their job, and their department. Customer needs and the overall good of the company come in second.

To correct this, deemphasize—but don't eliminate—individual department objectives and performance incentives. Instead, elevate company-wide results and the way each department plays a role in achieving those objectives.

For example, companies are in business to make money, regardless of what their corporate vision proclaims and their mission statement affirms. Look at how each department contributes to this, either directly or indirectly. It comes down to two activities: how much money they spend and how much money they bring in.

It's true that there are secondary metrics, often unique to each unit, that affect this. But to remove internal silos of control in your company, downplay the importance of the individual department measurements and instead look at overall company metrics.

Empower Agents to Best Serve Customers

Everyone knows to empower frontline people. Yet this is easier to say than to do. It's hard to let entry-level employees make decisions that cost money. Prohibiting them from doing so, however, has an even worse result. It costs customers.

When agents can't serve customers to the best of their ability to keep them happy, you end up losing their business, both now and in the future. Yes, sometimes empowered agents may overreach or make ill-advised decisions. Although undesirable, wouldn't it be better for them to do that than being kept from doing what's right for the customer and losing their business?

Integrate Communication Channels

With a multi-channel mindset, the goal is to provide contact options for customers. This requires sophisticated technology from vendors. Yet as end users of contact center platforms, make sure your implementation of the technology doesn't interfere with your ability to use it to its fullest and enjoy integrated communication channels.

Final Thoughts

These are big-picture considerations. You won't solve them quickly or easily, but you must pursue them if you want to provide the customer experience callers expect—a customer experience that retains them as your customers and doesn't shoo them away to your competitors.

WHAT KIND OF CUSTOMER EXPERIENCE DO YOU PROVIDE?

CUSTOMER EXPERIENCE IS MORE THAN A BUZZWORD—IT'S THE PATH TO SUCCESS

P eople love to share stories about their experiences when interacting with various companies. They post things online, which can have a far reach and may go viral. They also tell people face-to-face, which doesn't have the same reach but does have more impact.

The types of stories they like to share seldom fall in the category of typical. Instead, they pick outlier examples to tell others about. These are either interactions that went amazingly well or ones that went shockingly bad. The normal experiences are just too average to warrant much attention.

Therefore, they share extreme examples, which are far more fun to recount.

Negative Customer Experience

Most of the time, extreme customer experience examples are not positive ones. This may be because companies let us down more than they delight us. Or it could be because bad news garners more attention than good. If you doubt that, just watch the nightly news. Better yet, don't watch the news, and take my word for it. Rarely does the news include any feel-good stories, even though they do exist.

The more horrific the customer experience, the more interesting it seems, and the more it resonates with everyone who hears it. Revealing their awful experiences to others results in a shared experience of customer service gone awry. We've all been there. We all have stories. We tell them in person to our friends and families, and even strangers. We post them online, forming a permanent record for all to see how poorly a company treated us and how badly they wronged us.

When we vent, we feel better. This may be the only redress we'll ever receive for the wounds inflicted upon us. It doesn't correct the mistake, but it does lessen the sting—just a bit. Unfortunately, the company who stands as the villain in these stories can suffer much and suffer long, especially when the stories are posted online.

Positive Customer Experience

Much less common is a positive customer experience. They don't happen as often, and it's more likely they aren't so compelling to share. We gain more traction talking about our horrors than our delights. Even so, astounding customer experiences happen every day. It's just that we're less aware of them because people are less inclined to share them.

When told, these stories create a positive bond between us and the company. These tales create loyalty, and they produce repeat business. This is true for us, and it carries over to positively affect the people who hear our stories.

Just as negative customer experiences have a harmful impact on the company, positive customer experiences create the opposite.

Enhancing the Customer Experience

The customer service bar continually rises. What consumers considered excellent service five years ago is now the minimum standard. Furthermore, what was the acceptable standard a decade ago may have degraded to unacceptable now.

Just to stay even, we must seek to enhance the customer experience. And to gain ground, we must go beyond merely enhancing a customer's experience to overhauling it.

Final Thoughts

We don't achieve the needed changes by making incremental improvements. Tracking metrics and seeking to improve them seldom correlates to enhanced customer experiences. Instead, we need to rethink all we do in our customer-facing interactions. This includes knocking down internal silos of information and control, empowering agents to do what's right to best serve customers, and integrating communication channels.

As we do these things to overhaul our provision of customer service, we will enhance the customer experience. But remember, just enhancing the customer experience isn't the goal. Delighting customers and winning their loyalty is the objective we must seek.

$\sim$

In the following chapters, we'll look at some customer service experiences. I share these not to rant but to teach. May these illustrations inspire ideas to make your call center even better.

IS BEING EFFECTIVE GOOD ENOUGH?

DISCERN THE DIFFERENCE BETWEEN EFFECTIVE AND NOT-EFFECTIVE CUSTOMER SERVICE

I t doesn't matter if a call is answered in a modern contact center or by one person in a small, single-phone office. Customers evaluate every call the same way and expect the same outcomes. They compare each call with every other call and judge accordingly, regardless of who took the call or the technology behind it.

Consider three experiences I had in calling businesses without a call center. Then apply these lessons to your own operation.

1. A Husband-and-Wife Team

I needed to have a home inspection. A friend recommended a husband-and-wife team. He handled the inspections. She handled the office work. When I called, the quality of our interaction left me in awe. Not only was she professional, personal, and efficient, but she also excelled at high-level traits we value in the call center industry, such as tone, pacing, and pitch. It was as close to a perfect call as I've ever experienced.

When I had to call them to reschedule, she had a positive, no-problem attitude. Though I was inconveniencing them, there was no hint of that in her voice. Again, the results were impressive. Even more amazing is that she handled this call while in the car on her way to pick up one of her kids. I never would have known had she not apologized.

2. The Small Office

Another time, I called a local service company. I easily accomplished my objective of scheduling an appointment. Though the person wasn't skilled at customer service, I was pleased with her quick response.

Later I called back with a time-critical question. It was after hours, and she chastised me for calling in the evening. She did, however, address my question. Again, I was happy to have an answer.

The next day I had a follow-up question. This time my query was met with unrestrained impatience. She promised me a return call later that day and then changed it to "within twenty-four hours." The callback never came, but someone did show up two days later.

In the end, my frustration with her was offset by the professional work of her staff.

3. A Family Business

My third call was in response to a postcard sent by a lawn company. The wife answered the phone. She was friendly, although too casual for my taste. Still, we established a rapport. Yet her overly familiar demeanor, coupled with the absence of a hold button, caused me to shake my head.

In addition, I don't believe they even had an answering machine, because she always answered the phone, regardless of how many times it rang. The record was nine. Often self-deprecating, she nonetheless helped me on each call. In my many contacts, her call handling never changed. I give her high marks for consistency.

Her husband, who provided the service, was much the same in his conduct, overly friendly to the point of oversharing. Still, the finished product was done well and at a reasonable price.

Over time I grew to embrace them because they were nice people who produced the results I wanted.

Being Effective Is Essential

In the first and third cases, I deem my interactions as effective because I accomplished my desired purpose. Being effective means the caller's reason for calling is addressed, and the customer is pleased.

A rating of *effective* sets the minimal expectations for a call center. *Effective* stands as our baseline.

The second example, however, started out as effective but then degraded to not effective.

Not Effective

Calls that are not effective are failures. The callers' objectives aren't accomplished, or they aren't satisfied with the results. Too many enterprises run call centers that are *not effective*.

They give wrong information. Billing errors go uncorrected. Callbacks never occur. Customers must make repeated calls, but calls never move toward resolution.

Surpassing Effective

Other call centers offer the other extreme, being effective and then offering more. They are professional, accurate, consistent, and empathetic, with first-call resolution.

Final Thoughts

Whether you have one phone or hundreds of agents, first ensure you are *effective* in handling calls.

Then take things to a higher level by being more than effective. Become everything your callers hope for when they contact you.

YOUR COMPANY IS ONLY AS GOOD AS YOUR WEAKEST LINK

MAKE SURE YOUR CALL CENTER SUPPORTS WHAT YOUR COMPANY DOES

T oo much rain in too short of a time produced localized flooding. Coupled with some unusual factors, water gushed into our basement. It took four pumps, several hours of bailing, and the help of family and neighbors to stem the flow and remove the water faster than it entered.

Though things could have been much worse, every room in our lower level sustained water damage. As soon as the crisis was under control and I had gratefully thanked our rescuers, I turned my attention to the cleanup.

A Great First Call

I called the local office of a national firm that specializes in such things.

We got off to a good start. They answered their phone quickly and readily comprehended my situation. Though the person I talked to could have responded to my disaster with a hint of empathy rather than as a routine matter, she accomplished my main objective.

She confirmed that they knew just what to do to clean up the water. I decided to schedule service for the next morning when their rates were lower, and I could verify that the source of the problem was resolved. After all, there was no sense cleaning up twice.

The Second Call Was Not So Good

A few hours later I wondered if I should be doing something to prepare for them in the morning. I called back, assuming I'd reach an after-hours call center. I did not. I reached the same person I talked to earlier.

She was not pleased. "This is the emergency line."

"We're already scheduled for a team to come out at nine tomorrow, and I have a question," I explained.

"I don't have your records with me. They're at the office."

I wondered why she bothered answering the phone if she wasn't prepared to help. I pressed forward. "Is there anything I should do before they arrive?"

This seemed like a legitimate question. She felt otherwise. Though we failed to communicate, I did learn they would move furniture as needed. I gathered that it would be wise for us to move smaller items beforehand. By 11:00 p.m. my wife and I had our living room piled high with items from the basement. We fell into bed, exhausted.

Amazing Service

The team leader showed up at 8:35 the next morning, thoroughly explaining their procedure. The rest of the team arrived just before nine and went to work. When they finished by 2:00 p.m., we knew the extent of the damage.

Before he left, the team leader reiterated that normally someone would come out each day to assess the drying process and make sure there weren't any issues. But since they were extra busy because of the rains, it might not happen every day.

The Third Call Failure

Though I routinely monitored the two industrial dehumidifiers and twenty cyclone-strength fans strategically arranged in my basement, no one from their company did. I waited three days and finally called them.

"Your rep told me someone would check on the fans every day, but it's been three days and no one—"

"We're really busy," the woman interjected. "Someone will be out. It might not be today, but they will be out."

"I have some concerns. It's getting hot and—"

"It's supposed to get hot. That's how it's designed to work."

I didn't ask the rest of my questions. It seemed pointless.

"I'll make a note that you have *concerns*," she said with a hint of disdain, "but don't expect anyone until tomorrow."

My wife was incensed. "Call them back. Demand an answer."

"I don't want to make them mad. They might charge us more."

"Call back during lunch," she suggested. "Maybe you'll get someone else."

I shook my head. "I think they've forgotten who the customer is."

Though the team who cleaned our basement was thorough and professional, with an excellent team leader, their phone staff is their weak link, with their sub-par performance forming my overall impression of their service.

Final Thoughts

What must you do to make sure your call center is not the weak link in your operation? What are some ways you can keep your staff aware of who the customer is?

CUSTOMER SERVICE: YOU CAN DO IT THE EASY WAY OR THE HARD WAY

STRIVE TO SERVE CUSTOMERS, NOT IRRITATE THEM

W hen my wife and I moved, some aspects went smoothly, while others were not so good.

Part of moving is canceling services and changing mailing addresses. Each task is a customer service opportunity. Some companies excel at this, while others struggle, which requires repeat calls. This extra effort impacts both customers and employees.

Easy

Changing our address was the easiest with most individuals and companies. I just emailed them.

When my wife called to cancel the garbage service, the rep took the information with ease and the refund check arrived a couple weeks later.

The gas utility was likewise easy: One call and done. Our final bill arrived soon after.

Not So Easy

The electric company was more involved. The phone call went well, but the subsequent bill didn't show the service as canceled. It took a second phone call to fully resolve the problem. This meant double the work for me and them.

Updating addresses for magazine subscriptions was a time-consuming online process and not always straightforward, so a couple of cases resulted in duplicate mailings.

Infuriating

Though we no longer have a landline phone, we did then. A large regional carrier provided our home phone.

When I called to cancel this number, the rep took my order and left me feeling confident. They disconnected the line within an hour, but the new-number recording wasn't activated. A second rep told me the first one placed the order wrong. It would take twelve hours for the change to go through. By the weekend, there was still no recording. After a third call, customer service said the order was still wrong, but they couldn't fix it because I was no longer a customer. The fourth call, this one to the repair department, resulted in the same story. A fifth call on Monday produced only frustration. After repeated begging, the rep transferred me to a supervisor. A few minutes later, the recording was working.

That left my business line, which was bundled with internet access and video, courtesy of a local telephone company. A small operation, these folks know how to service customers. Though their methods aren't always professional, they are effective.

Placing the cancelation was easy, but they didn't offer new-number recordings. When I insisted, the rep put me on hold to consult with their head engineer. His response shocked me: Their switch couldn't do a new-number recording. The solution I eventually settled for was to keep the phone number active and have calls forwarded to my new number until I could notify everyone. This solution took multiple calls, callbacks, and consultations, consuming way too much of my time and theirs.

With our credit union, I updated our address online, but our bank didn't allow that. A call to their main office left me frustrated. I had to go to their nearest branch, now sixty miles away, to fill out a form. This isn't customer service; it's customer disservice.

Final Thoughts

In your contact center, look for ways to prevent repeat calls, reduce customer frustrations, and avoid customer disservice like I encountered with my bank. Doing so will delight callers, save your staff from extra work and angry follow-up calls, and make everyone happy.

CUSTOMER SERVICE RECOVERY
THE FINAL IMPRESSION YOU MAKE IS OFTEN
THE LASTING ONE

I once experienced poor customer service and great customer service. Both happened the same day and from the same organization.

Several years ago, I banked with a small local provider. They had a main office and two branches. For over a decade, I always went to the nearest branch. When I made a deposit, I used the lobby. This wasn't because I had an aversion to drive-through convenience but because face-to-face was more personal. I wanted to know those who handled my money and—more importantly—I wanted them to know me.

One day I needed to check on a transaction. I went online—or I attempted to. My login was denied. Next, I tried bank-by-phone. Invalid password.

Training Shortfall

I then called the main office, where the records are kept.

Though the woman understood my request, she took a long time to find the answer. Lengthy hold times were part of the process. I received the needed information, and she was about to hang up.

I stopped her. "I can't log in to online banking or bank-by-phone." I gave her the details. Once she realized I wished to resolve these issues, she put me on hold again.

It's Your Fault

She returned, telling me what to do when I've forgotten my password. "I didn't forget it," I clarified. "It's just not working." She did some typing and conferred with her coworker, this time without putting me on hold. She was confused.

She instructed me to try again and then informed me I was locked out because of too many failed login attempts.

"I was just doing what you told me to do."

You Have To

There was more conferring with her coworker. Then, her next words jarred me. "To reset your password, you have to fax or mail written authorization." She couldn't help me until I did.

"That is most disappointing," I replied, and we ended the call.

This was not my first service issue of the day, and I began silently grousing. I don't *have* to do anything.

Making It Right

I was still stewing when the phone rang. It was the branch manager where I usually bank. We're on a first-name basis. She apologized for her coworker's miscommunication. For security purposes, the bank had recently required every customer to change their passwords. We would be locked out until we did. Apparently, the person I talked to had been hurriedly brought in to address the deluge of phone calls that resulted from this mandate.

In the time it took her to explain this, the manager had reset my password, and I could log in. We'd deal with the paperwork later.

The manager's exemplary response overcame the disappointing shortcomings of her coworker. It was a stellar example of customer service recovery.

Final Thoughts

The first goal should be to not cause customer angst in the first place. The next best thing is to recover smartly from it when you do.

TECHNOLOGY

Technology is the backbone of today's call center. Gone are the days when all you needed was a multi-line telephone, a headset, and a message pad or order form.

The modern call center runs on technology. It's a technology-intensive enterprise (along with being a labor-intensive one too).

Call center technology receives and routes calls, provides apps and databases to facilitate agent work, and allows for distributed opportunities that wouldn't otherwise be available.

Without the right technology tools in place, today's call center would falter.

WHAT'S YOUR TECHNOLOGY STRATEGY?

DETERMINE IF YOUR CALL CENTER PLATFORM SHOULD BE ONSITE OR ONLINE

T raditionally, call centers have installed their systems onsite. Yet technological advances have made off-site systems—online solutions—viable options that offer compelling advantages.

Onsite System

Having premise-based equipment allows for greater control. But with control comes responsibility. This includes maintenance, database backups, software updates, spare parts inventory, disaster recovery, backup power, and IT staff.

Financially, onsite software and equipment represents a tangible asset, which is a capitalized purchase and a depreciated line item on the balance sheet. While there are usually some ongoing costs, they're minor in comparison. Onsite equipment doesn't require internet access to operate—but with the increased prevalence of VoIP and many forms of contact occurring over the internet, this truth becomes a nonissue.

Although vendor stability is a concern for both options, with onsite installations, there is at least the potential for the call center to continue operating if the vendor fails. This is not so with the alternative.

Online System

Off-site solutions represent a new way of provisioning a call center. With it, the responsibility to install and maintain equipment is removed, but along with it goes the associated control. There is no capital purchase or depreciation, with the only costs being a predictable, ongoing monthly expense, which is proportionate to actual usage. This appears as an income statement item and doesn't impact the balance sheet.

Online solutions also offer the flexibility to ramp up and ramp down as needed. Operations may be deployed anywhere that has reliable internet access, which can easily accommodate remote agents.

There are two chief concerns, however, with online solutions. One is the requirement of a stable internet connection for both the call center and remote agents. Without internet access, the call center is effectively down.

The other concern is with the vendor. Do they provide

always-on, fully redundant, carrier-grade stability, with 24/7 tech support and IT staff? Are they financially viable to offer online service for the long term? If they stumble or fail, the call center immediately suffers the same fate.

For much of the call center industry's decades-long history, onsite equipment was the only option. Some centers continue to pursue this approach, not because they've examined the alternative, but because that's how it's always been. They see no point in changing.

Equally unacceptable are those call centers that race headlong into online solutions, merely to follow the trend. They dismiss the alternative simply because it's the old way of doing things. An unexamined strategy is really no strategy at all.

Final Thoughts

Neither approach is universally right. Both have merits. Both have disadvantages. Take a careful look at the pros and cons of each option. Then make a strategic decision on which one is the best for you and your call center. Your future may be at stake.

SOCIAL MEDIA AND THE CONTACT CENTER

CONSIDER WAYS TO SHIFT FROM CALLS TO CONTACTS

S hould your call center become a contact center to handle social media for your organization or clients? Perhaps you've already made the shift, but you desire to do so with greater ease and effectiveness. Alternately, the idea of social media as part of your contact center mix may present an overwhelming challenge that you'd prefer not to touch.

Let the Past Illuminate the Present

Regardless of your perspective, looking at the past can shine a light to better illuminate the present, providing hope for the haggard and vision for the cautious.

First there were calls, whether inbound or outbound. The answering of ringing phones and the dialing of digits were the sole purpose of call centers for decades. Aside from some operations that may have also handled faxes and snail mail, call centers were just that, centralized workplaces where agents processed calls. But faxes came and went, as did the art of letter writing, both giving way to the simplicity and speed of a new technology, email.

Email ushered in a philosophical transition in name from call center to contact center, following the increased communication options available to consumers. This revised name more fully embraced the expanded contact options of the quintessential call center. Not far behind email came text chat, a third customer communication channel for the contact center to consider.

In the early days, agents often had to try to handle all three. This was without the benefit of universal queues or even integrated tools. While email could be batched—providing the delay wasn't too great—chat carried with it the expectation of a near real-time response. Over time, email and chat platforms began to interface with call center switches, eventually giving way to full integration. This allowed for the universal queue, which forever prevented a phone call and a chat from arriving simultaneously while an agent worked on an email.

While some contact centers continue to operate in this mode, with agents switching between calls, chats, and emails as needed, other operations segregated these tasks, allowing agents to specialize on one function, sometimes even at dedicated operation centers.

The Implications for Social Media

What does all this have to do with social media?

Just as in the early days of contact centers trying to handle email and chat with kludged-together tools that didn't play well with each other, processing social media comments and posts within the contact center is likewise at its awkward stage. Yes, vendors—due in part to what they learned with email and chat—are doing much better today than they did back then.

Still, further progress is needed, though it's occurring rapidly. If you've not recently looked at all the social media tools and solutions for call centers, you're likely working with an old understanding of what is available. Over time, these systems and software solutions will function better within the contact center and fully integrate with the existing infrastructure—just as it happened with email and chat solutions.

There is also a new twist, however, that social media provides. While phone calls, emails, and chats all require a need to respond to each one individually, not all social media carries that expectation. True, customer service communications from social media platforms require a response, but other posts, comments, and likes don't warrant a personal agent-generated reaction.

Instead, some social media activity rightly needs to be aggregated, considered as a group rather than in parts. This means being able to spot trends early on and detect potentially viral posts before they become fully inflamed. This allows contact center agents to respond quickly—or escalate the situation if needed—before an issue gets out of control and becomes unmanageable.

This is proactive customer service on a higher level.

Final Thoughts

Opportunities abound for today's contact center. The latest one takes a leading role in taming social media channels to turn them into more ways to serve customers and resolve problems.

CONSIDER HOW ARTIFICIAL INTELLIGENCE CAN HELP US IN THE CALL CENTER

WE SHOULD EMBRACE AI AS A USEFUL TOOLSET AND NOT FEAR IT

Artificial intelligence (AI) is not a fad that will go away. It's a fundamental shift in how all businesses—and every person—will function in the future. And though you may not yet realize it, that future is here. Even if you haven't openly invited artificial intelligence into your call center operation, it's already arrived, albeit via circuitous points of entry.

Many people already use artificial intelligence and don't even know it. AI helps us draft email messages and compose text communications. It facilitates online searches. And AI targets advertising—both the ads we receive and the ones we send. AI also works to keep us secure online. In doing these things—and many more—AI saves us time and helps us be more productive.

We'll talk about artificial intelligence in general terms

because the specifics will be out of date within days. That's how fast AI technology is advancing.

Consider these areas where artificial intelligence can help us in our call centers to do our jobs more effectively and efficiently.

Management Tools

Artificial intelligence can help us manage our call center operation and our call center staff with greater ease.

One area, for example, is in quality assurance (QA). AI can perform a QA analysis on our agents to measure the overall effectiveness of their work. This not only removes the tedium of doing so manually, but it also makes sure it's done and not put off. And it also does so for every call, which isn't feasible from a human standpoint.

Interdepartmental Interactions

While we typically think of how artificial intelligence can facilitate interactions with customers and callers, we shouldn't overlook its potential to assist in internal communication and collaboration between departments.

Consider a customer service event and the ripple effects its resolution causes. AI could serve to notify all stakeholders and even support their work that relates to it. As appropriate, AI could trigger a billing adjustment, escalate a QA report, reprogram an account, update a service record, and so on.

Agent Support

Though artificial intelligence could—and one day may—replace much of the human involvement in call center work, we're best to view it now as supporting our agents so they can do their jobs better and faster. The above mentioned—and presently available—AI-assisted email and text messaging tools are an obvious start. Though these still require agent involvement or agent approval, imagine being able to compose these messages in less time and with greater accuracy.

Customer-Facing Communications

When many people think of AI in the call center, they envision frustrating bots that hamper effective communication and thwart timely resolution. Though reports of AI that took the wrong path confirm just this, it doesn't need to be —and shouldn't be—the case.

Chat bots are an obvious example. Though they don't presently function well as a holistic solution and can make a mess of unusual situations, they work great as a front-end resource to solve basic problems, gather key information, and appropriately route customer requests to agents.

Now consider the same concept occurring with telephone calls. Then imagine text-to-speech technology producing canned responses in each operator's voice and indistinguishable from their own speech when they need to take over a call.

Final Thoughts

We need not fear the forward march of artificial intelligence. There is much we can do to make our call centers function faster and more accurately than ever before. We'll benefit and so will those we interact with, both inside our organization and without.

Artificial intelligence can help us, if only we will let it.

WILL CUSTOMER SERVICE CHATBOTS RUIN CUSTOMER SERVICE?

KEEP TECHNOLOGY FROM INFILTRATING AND TAKING OVER THE CONTACT CENTER

B ots, sometimes called chatbots, are applications used to automate responses to social media and online inquiries. The purpose of bots is to speed answers to customer information requests. And they do this automatically. They're programs, after all.

They can accomplish in a fraction of a second what it might take a person several minutes to handle—or even longer if the message gets stuck in a lengthy queue.

Chatbots Today

Chatbots respond quickly, expedite communication, and relieve customer service staff from handling basic inquiries. What does this mean to contact centers and their staff?

Could chatbots signal the end of the contact center as we know it?

Although it's easy to imagine these chatbot programs one day taking over a contact center and sending all agents home because they have no work left to do, this is unlikely. Go through the history of the call center industry. Every year or two we see some new technology coming along that carries the threat of devastating the call center. So far, it's never happened.

Although emerging technologies change how the call center operates, in most cases these innovations have opened new opportunities to better serve customers and provide more work for agents. Historically, these technologies have not been disruptive but enabling.

Bots are not a threat to contact center agents. They're a tool to aid communication, assist agents, and speed answers to customers. Just as web self-service and FAQ sections on websites help customers resolve problems, so too can self-learning bots.

Though online self-service was once heralded as the end of contact centers, this proved false, with frustrated users demanding to talk with people to resolve their most pressing problems. Bots will have the same effect.

Yet, as the saying goes, "To err is human, but to really foul things up requires a computer." Bots could accomplish this too. They are, after all, self-learning. What if they learn the wrong thing? It happens. What if they reach an errant conclusion and then perpetuate it, inflicting their misinformation on thousands of people?

Who will suffer the fallout? The contact center will, as agents field calls, emails, and text messages from confused customers led astray by erroneous bots.

Who's going to fix the mess? Contact center agents, that's who: real people solving big problems caused by well-meaning technology run amuck. This possibility, though likely, should only happen in isolated cases.

Ever Learning and Evolving

Yet there's a bigger issue at stake. Unlike a typical computer application that can only do what it was programmed to do, bots have an element of artificial intelligence built into them. They can grow, they can evolve, and they can adapt.

They could take over!

Though this may sound like an intriguing plot for a sci-fi thriller, it's a call center possibility, even if far-fetched. But if bots take over and turn customer service into a nightmare, it will be the contact center agents who come to the rescue and save us all!

My attempts at humor aside, bots present more opportunities than threats.

We need to implement them to better serve our customers. Let the bots do the easy things—just as we expect from self-service, FAQs, and interactive voice response—so that contact center agents can focus their attention on the more challenging inquiries.

Final Thoughts

Bots will take some of the drudgery out of routine contact center chores and defer to real people for the more challenging work.

Chatbots will not likely ruin the contact center industry. They will empower it to become more.

CHATBOTS SHOULD LEARN FROM THE ERRORS OF IVR

DON'T LET CHATBOTS BE LIKE IVR, WHICH EARNED CUSTOMER IRE THROUGH POOR IMPLEMENTATION

I don't often use text chat because I find a phone call is faster and more thorough. Recently I made an exception and learned a valuable lesson.

The email said my new statement was available online. I might be one of the few people who still download and review online statements, but that's what I do. So I logged in and navigated to the right page. I clicked on the link for my most recent statement, but it brought up last month's. With more navigation, I found a list of all my statements. Alas, my current statement wasn't there.

The Bot

About this time a chat invitation popped up. "I see you've been notified your new statement is available. Can I help you?"

Without giving it enough thought, I typed in, "I can't download my statement."

Immediately I received a reply. "Here are two resources that might help you."

By the titles of these links, I knew they pointed in the wrong direction, telling me what I already knew. I tried again. "No, my current statement isn't available."

Again, the chatbot responded immediately. "Here are three links that might help you resolve the problem."

Once again, the links wouldn't help. What started as an amusing experience with technology was becoming exasperating. Then I typed, "Can I talk with a person?"

The bot responded immediately, "I can help you."

Obviously, the bot wasn't interested in connecting me with a real person. I typed in what I thought: "You're worthless." (Though I've never said that to a person, I often say that to technology.)

But before I could close the chat window, I got another message. "Let me connect you with a representative."

The Person

With a potential for help only seconds away, I stuck around. A half minute later, Lisa popped up in the chat window.

Unfortunately, my failed chatbot experience agitated me, like what happens after futile interaction with IVR (interactive voice response). At this point, emotion, rather than logic, dictated my first question. "Are you a person or a bot?"

Lisa assured me she was a real person. She then tried to help. She had me try a different method to get to my statement, but that didn't work either. I pasted the error message into the chat window for her to see. Then she had me try a different browser. I got the same results.

The Problem

As we continued, I recalled a problem with my credit union a few years ago. They would often email me that my statement was available, even though the department responsible for putting it online hadn't finished their work. The two groups weren't communicating.

I realized that the same thing had happened with this company. Expecting the statement to be online by a certain time, the email group sent out a notice, unaware that the statement wasn't available.

This, of course, brings up another all-too-common scenario: a company causes needless customer service activity by their own actions. But that's a topic we've already covered.

Final Thoughts

The point here is that chatbots are part of exciting technologies that can help call centers better serve customers, as well as help agents do their job better. Yet the improper application of chatbot technology threatens its utility by alienating the customers it's supposed to help.

This is exactly what happened with the introduction of IVR, and that technology never recovered from its negative public perception. May chatbots have a different outcome. Both the call center and its customers need this one to be a win.

STRATEGIC CALL DISTRIBUTION
THE DELICATE BALANCE BETWEEN IDEALISM AND PRAGMATISM

I will admit it—I have a propensity toward idealism. I think that life should be fair and that everyone, regardless of position or past, ought to be granted equality of opportunity.

This perspective causes me to advocate impartiality when distributing calls in the call center, with each call handled in the order in which it was received, without distinction of origin or predetermined importance. It seems, however, that few call centers concur. In fact, pragmatism and reality dictate a different course.

Reasons to Distinguish

The first deviation is often to give primacy to sales. After all, the efficiency at which these calls are handled will form the callers' perception of the level of service provided. It's this perception that attracts new business, thereby affecting profitability.

The second departure from call equality is also self-imposed, whereby certain account groups are deemed more important than others. Although the determining factors vary—caller urgency, projected dollar value of the call, or type of service provided—the results are a definite segregation of callers into a tiered call-distribution scheme.

A third divergence is more insidious. This results from a natural reaction to the *squeaky wheel* syndrome. It's when the chronic complainers and excessively demanding are given a higher call priority to appease their sense of self-worth or to mitigate their criticisms about service level.

This is the most ominous departure from ideal call distribution—and the most self-defeating. Examine callers in this category. We've already defined them to be overly critical and implied them to be frequent users—and abusers—of customer service resources.

Now dig a bit further. How do these callers treat your staff? Are they pleasant and a joy to talk to or do they challenge, threaten, and denigrate your agents with each interaction? Are these the customers who take the joy out of your agents' work and reduce staff to tears? I suspect this might be the case.

If this is not enough, now look at their profitability level. If they badger both agent and supervisor, they likely treat accounting the same way, extracting credits, demanding discounts, and insisting on other monetary concessions under the pretext of "poor service."

The conclusion is inescapable. These customers receive the highest level of service, treat your staff the worst, and are unprofitable. Giving them expedited service is masochistic behavior. Stop it.

The Opposite Approach

I propose—in partial jest but with thought-provoking seriousness—that you consider a different model. If you deviate from the idealism of universal call distribution, do so with thoughtful analysis and self-serving diligence.

First, implement call distribution based on profitability. Perform a profitability analysis of customers. The most profitable ones should receive the highest priority in call distribution, and the least profitable ones, the lowest consideration.

What I've advocated is likely a reversal of your current call-distribution configuration, thinking tactically instead of being reactionary.

If that sounds like fun—as well as being a good business strategy—take the concept to the next level.

First, survey your staff. Which customers do they like, and which cause undue consternation? For the nice customers—those who treat your staff with respect—move them higher in the call-distribution hierarchy. After all, these customers make your staff happy, and a happy staff is an effective staff. Conversely, those customers your staff cites for their undesirable characteristics, move them lower.

Next, check with accounting. Look at payment history. Some customers consistently pay soon after getting your invoice. Others pay by the due date. A few may habitually stretch your terms to forty-five or sixty days.

Again, modify your call-handling priorities based on payment history. Move those who pay immediately up one level. And those who pay late, move down a notch. But those who present a constant challenge to collect, move down more. After all, they may eventually leave you with an uncollectable debt, so why not give better-paying customers a higher priority?

Implementation

If this discussion has you excited, wonderful. If your mind is churning with revolutionary ideas to change call-handling priorities, great.

Yet don't implement these radical changes all at once, or even too quickly. The shock to your customer base might be more than they—or your business—can tolerate.

Instead, begin to think strategically about call distribution, making small, incremental steps to prioritize calls from your best customers. The change will be extraordinary.

Final Thoughts

As you implement technology in your call center, be aware of the options of how it's configured and employed. Engineering may have one perspective, customer service another, and leadership a third.

Pursue a strategic approach to balance everyone's perspective and produce the most beneficial outcome.

IS THE FUTURE YOUR FRIEND OR FOE?

BE READY FOR TECHNOLOGY TO REVOLUTIONIZE YOUR CALL CENTER

As a writer about call centers, I see interesting parallels between writing and call centers. Technology affects both. One area is AI. Though we'll use that as an illustration, the discussion applies to all technology.

Futurists in the writing community talk about how AI will arise as a disruptive force. Indeed, the disruption has already begun, with AI producing noteworthy content. Some writers deny AI and consider it a pipe dream. Others see it as the end of writing as we know it and a threat to their livelihood. Last are those, like me, who see AI as a tool that will help us write more effectively. Yes, writing as we know it today will change dramatically, but that change is something to embrace.

In similar fashion, AI impacts the call center industry,

and the reactions to AI in the call center space are much the same as in the writing world.

Blissfully Unaware

Some people in the call center industry have no awareness of the burgeoning developments with AI and how it will dramatically change call centers and the provision of customer care. They view AI as the topic for sci-fi movies, scientific labs, and a far-off future—one that will occur long after they no longer care.

Instead, they focus on the day-to-day urgencies of hiring, training, and scheduling agents. They look at metrics such as first-call resolution, speed of answer, and average call length. They consider the number of calls in queue, time in queue, and abandonment rate. And their world focuses on resolving customer complaints. There's nothing wrong with these worthy pursuits, but it keeps them from considering tomorrow and embracing the future.

Deny It's a Threat

Others acknowledge the existence of AI, but they don't see how it could help call centers serve customers better. They deny its utility.

If anything, they assume AI will make customer service harder and therefore perpetuate the need for live agents. To them, AI is another call-center fad that will receive a lot of hype for a few years and then fade. Their response is to maintain the status quo.

Fearful Over the Future

Next are the Luddites, those who oppose adding more technology. Though some call centers embrace technology much more than others, every call center has some degree of tech in its infrastructure and operations. These people have formed a comfortable truce with the tools they use, but they don't want any more of it.

They have enough technology already in place, and everything works fine, thank you very much. More tools, such as AI-powered solutions, make them shudder. They fear self-learning programs will take over the call center and eliminate jobs.

Embrace It with Optimism

The final group looks at AI as an intriguing call-center solution. Yes, it will fundamentally change how call centers operate. And this transformation could happen much sooner than most people suspect. Yet instead of fearing uncertainty over the unknown, these forward-thinking futurists welcome AI as a smart solution to address many of today's call-center challenges.

Yes, in some cases, AI will replace jobs, just as voicemail, automated attendants, and IVR have done in the past. In other cases, AI will assist call center agents, helping them work more effectively and efficiently. This will occur just as today's tools have improved the results produced from past technologies.

Then, now, and in the future, the customer benefits by realizing enhanced outcomes.

Final Thoughts

As with AI, thanks to all innovative technology, future call centers won't need to hire as many agents. And those you do hire will benefit by having technology tools to guide their work.

These employees will find their call center job less dreary and more invigorating. The days of routinely shuffling through repetitive calls will end, replaced with variety in handling challenging calls that technology can't address. This will provide the opportunity to excel in call-center work as never before.

What role will you let technology play in your call center?

STRATEGY

As we wrap up our discussion on call center success, we'll address the all-important area of strategy. Though it's easy to go from call to call, day to day, and year to year doing the same thing you've always done, the reality is you need a focused strategy to guide what you do.

Many books address strategy from a theoretical standpoint, so we'll not repeat that information here. Instead, we'll look at some practical strategic elements for your consideration.

Use these chapters to inform your own call center strategy, driving you toward success.

A BRIEF HISTORY OF CALL CENTERS VERSUS SELF-SERVICE

EMBRACE THE CALL CENTER AS A BUSINESS STRATEGY

The call center has had its share of detractors over the years, from businesses that dismissed it as an unnecessary cost to consumers quick to voice their frustrations to politicians who want to fix it. (Actually, most politicians just want the support of frustrated voters.)

Yesterday's Failure

One big salvo against the call center came during the dot-com bubble, which advocated online self-support in lieu of call center customer service. It was good in concept: a scalable solution with minimal labor expenses. The only problem was that self-support didn't work all that well. With too many wrong answers and not enough good ones, self-support meant no support for most people.

The belief that end users didn't need customer service support mostly died when the dot-com bubble burst. Call centers were needed, and many businesses restored them. But many focused only on the profitability and viewed the call center as a cost center, an expense to be controlled.

Many businesses outsourced their call centers to other countries to tap into lower-cost labor markets and save money. They went offshore to the lowest cost provider. The results were disastrous. It's not that offshore call centers are bad, but when the focus is on cost containment over quality service, callers are bound to complain. And complain they did: to the businesses, to each other on social media, and to their elected officials.

Many offshore call centers returned onshore, and most of the rest focused on improved quality over lower costs. Everyone won—well, almost everyone. Most in the younger generations—reared on a self-service mindset and conditioned to experience low-quality phone support—wrote off the call center and never returned. Picking up the phone became their last option, and we trained them to think this way.

This is the current reality of customer service.

Today's Dichotomy

In general, older customers tend to expect they can call a phone number to talk to a real person who will profession-ally, accurately, and quickly address the reason for their call.

This isn't an unrealistic expectation. It's good customer service.

If you fail to deliver, they may go grumbling to the self-service route—or they may not even try. More likely they'll complain to any person who will listen. And if you disappoint them severely enough, they'll stop doing business with you and go to your competitor.

Conversely, younger customers tend to want to "figure it out myself." They'll go the self-service route. Bolstering this is the fact that they don't like talking on the phone, and they don't think your reps will be able to help them.

Your self-serve options better be ready to address their concerns. If you fall short, they may grumble as they call you—or they may not. More likely they'll complain online to anyone who will listen. This amplifies their frustration and multiplies the negativity toward your brand. And if you disappoint them severely enough, they'll also stop doing business with you and go to your competitor.

Yet I see many reasons for call center optimism.

With the call center becoming the contact center—handling email, text, and social media—and advanced technology enhancing self-service, the two will meet in the middle.

Your contact center staff will provide non-phone support to those who can't find their answer through self-service but are loath to pick up the phone. And your self-service options will grow and mature to help customers more effectively, while providing a real person to intervene when needed.

In doing so, the call center and self-serve solution will merge to become an all-encompassing, comprehensive customer service department to meet the needs of all your customers.

Final Thoughts

Embrace the importance of having people help people—regardless of the customer's entry point into your system and the channel used.

It's a sound strategy.

ARE YOU A CALL CENTER OR A CONTACT CENTER?
CONSIDER THE STRATEGIC IMPLICATIONS

The term *call center* is a descriptive one. It's a centralized place that receives or makes phone calls. This label has served us well for several decades.

Nevertheless, most call centers have expanded their service offerings to handle more than just telephone calls. They may also process email and text messages, as well as perform various social media functions. Some also handle faxes and snail mail. These go beyond the meaning of the word *call*, with *contact* being a more inclusive description. Hence, we get the term *contact center*.

Yet the word *center* emerges as a misnomer, since many call or contact centers have decentralized their operation. Instead, they have a distributed workforce, with staff no longer in a single location.

Effective Communications

More people comprehend *call center* than *contact center*—even if it evokes a negative reaction. Despite *call center* no longer serving as an accurate label, it's the best way to communicate with people outside the industry. When effective communication is the goal, using the term *call center* is the best way to accomplish that.

Strategic

Those who advocate *contact center* may be purists who want to use an accurate label. Even so, they're only halfway there and must figure out how to deal with the no-longer-accurate use of *center*.

One reason to use *contact center* instead of *call center* is to emphasize that the operation handles multiple forms of communication beyond phone calls. This helps the operation emphasize the scope of its work to stakeholders and better guide strategic planning.

Branding

In the outsourcing area, most people who insist on the label *contact center* do so for branding purposes. They may want to distance their brand from the negative public opinion about call centers, courtesy of the players who did it badly and ruined the industry's reputation.

But unless everyone in the industry decides to be ethical and do their work with excellence, the *contact center* label risks becoming just as toxic as *call center* to those who've had bad experiences.

Regardless, most operations already cover multiple communication channels, so companies who want to hire a call or contact center already know the labels don't matter anymore. They can get the service they want regardless of the name the provider uses.

Final Thoughts

The next time your organization dives into the "Are we a call center or a contact center?" debate, shift the focus from words to action. Pursue initiatives that will produce quality service and heighten your company's reputation, along with the overall industry.

That's what matters.

IS YOUR CALL CENTER A PROFIT CENTER OR A COST CENTER?

POSITIONING YOURSELF TO DRIVE REVENUE WILL PROVIDE BUDGET SUCCESS

A corporate marketing manager told me their call center was their most cost-effective form of marketing, offering the highest return on investment (ROI). It was a profit center, bringing money into the business.

Further shocking was learning that the entire call center operation fell under the budget of the marketing department. I imagine the call center director had little trouble getting the appropriate budget each year to operate the call center.

The Downside of Being a Cost Center

The opposite of being a profit center is being a cost center. A cost center requires more money to run than it generates.

This is not an ideal position for a call center.

If upper management views your operation as a cost center, they'll see your line item on their budget as an expense to control and decrease whenever possible. This results in a scarcity of funds and makes it hard to operate as needed to produce the best outcomes for customers.

Each new budget cycle produces a predictable challenge of fighting to maintain the status quo of your funds. And receiving approval for additional expenditures on software, services, and initiatives to better serve callers looms as a formidable challenge.

If this is your reality, I feel for you. But there is hope: reposition your call center as a profit center.

The Benefits of Being a Profit Center

If your call center generates revenue—either directly or indirectly—you stand a much better chance of coming out on the plus side for each year's budget.

If you provide a product, it's easy to make your case. You start by tracking sales, which you then use to offset the cost of your operation. Any expense that produces more sales becomes an easy request to justify.

Even if your call center doesn't directly close sales or take phone orders, you can still work to establish yourself as a profit center. It just takes a bit more effort.

How to Become a Profit Center

Start making this transition by identifying the ways you contribute to the revenue stream of your company. For example, each time you refer a prospect to sales, what's the value of that connection? Even more significant, what's the lifetime value of that new customer to your business? Suddenly that single phone call has a value of hundreds or thousands of dollars, maybe more.

What about setting sales appointments? Each time you schedule a sales meeting, what's its revenue potential? And often that initial appointment leads to subsequent sales and revenue. Though these additional interactions may not go through your call center, the subsequent outcomes wouldn't have occurred had you not secured the first one.

Without your call center, these things—sales and appointments—would not have happened. As such, you deserve credit for the critical role your call center played in bringing this new business—and revenue—into your company.

Final Thoughts

Start tracking these types of revenue-producing transactions. But don't just note the number of calls. Instead, report the immediate value and long-term revenue potential from each of these interactions.

In doing so you'll help shift your call center operation from a cost center to a profit center. And this will make a huge difference when it comes time to negotiate next year's budget.

DEVELOPING YOUR CALLBACK STRATEGY
DESIGN A CALLBACK STRATEGY THAT WORKS FOR YOU AND YOUR CALLERS

Though not every caller will use it, many appreciate the option to have you call them back instead of waiting on hold. As with any technology, callback strategy evolves.

Therefore, look at what you're currently doing to see if it still makes sense. Ensure it best facilitates communication between you and your callers.

Here are some questions to ask yourself as you look at developing your callback strategy. Follow these tips to achieve the best results.

Where Are They in the Queue?

A much-appreciated courtesy to give callers as they wait to talk to you is to let them know where they are in the queue.

In short, how long before they can talk to somebody?

This is vital information for a caller to know as they contemplate whether they should accept your offer of receiving a callback. If they can stay in queue and talk with someone in a minute or two, most people will want to wait. But if the delay is longer, many will opt for a callback.

What about Your Callback Queue?

Once someone asks for a callback, do they go into a separate queue or is it integrated with your new-call queue? Having separate queues allows for dedicated callback agents. Most agents will take new calls and the rest will handle callbacks.

Alternately, you can prioritize callbacks, moving them ahead of new calls. Or you can prioritize new calls, moving callbacks to the end of the line.

There isn't one universally right answer here, but there is a right answer for *your* operation. Just be sure to make an informed decision.

What Is Your Maximum Callback Time?

Another consideration is if you want to set a maximum threshold to make the callback. If you wait too long, your customer may no longer care, and you may have lost their business. Yet trying to place callbacks too quickly could jeopardize new-call responsiveness.

Balance what's reasonable for the caller and feasible for your operation.

What If You Can't Make the Callback the Same Day?

Also develop a policy for what you'll do if there are still pending callbacks to make at the end of the workday. Will you have staff stay late to make sure they happen? Or will you roll those pending callbacks into the next day? If you do this, consider your customers' reactions. They may not be good.

What If the Customer Isn't Available When You Call?

Your customers are busy people, too, perhaps as busy as your agents. There's a chance that when you call them back, they won't be available. What should you do?

The worst reaction is to hang up and forget about them. You could leave a message and let them call you back. Or you could hang up and call them back in a few minutes. Even better would be to leave a message *and* call them back.

Should You Allow Scheduled Callbacks?

Putting callbacks in a general queue or having a separate callback queue supports optimum call center efficiency. But what about your customers waiting for you to call them back? Though it may be more work for you to let them schedule callbacks, it's a smart customer-centric move. Just be sure that someone calls them back when they request it.

Final Thoughts

Offering to call customers back when you get busy is a feature that consumers increasingly expect call centers to offer. If they desire it and you don't provide it, you'll disappoint them. Disappoint them too often and they'll take their business elsewhere.

Instead, follow these suggestions in developing your callback strategy, and you'll score with your callers.

IT ALL DEPENDS

BEWARE OF UNWISE COMPARISONS THAT COULD LEAD YOU ASTRAY

I n business school, I learned that the answer to many questions was "It all depends." The same response often holds true for the call center, where the answer to many questions is "It all depends."

Occupancy Rates

First, it depends on the form and function of the call center. Centers that handle multiple contact points, such as phone calls, email, and text, realize a higher occupancy rate and enjoy greater productivity. (Occupancy is the amount of time agents spend working with callers compared to the time they're available to work.)

However, the size of the call center is the main variable affecting operational efficacy. I've seen occupancy rates as low as the mid-twenties to as high as the mid-nineties and everywhere in between.

In certain circumstances, any of these results could be the appropriate occupancy rate. Conversely, it could also be the wrong one. The key reason hinges on the primary reason for call centers in the first place: economies of scale.

Consider the following scenarios.

The smallest call center, or at least the smallest *staffed* one, will have one person working per shift, 24/7. There will be times when this solitary agent is extremely busy (peak daytime traffic) and other times with virtually no calls (the middle of the night). As such, occupancy rates will vary greatly throughout the day, from quite low to moderately high.

Also, whether you blame it on Erlang traffic projections or Murphy's law, there is also a tendency for calls to bunch up. In a call center, the additional calls go into the queue and wait for the *next available agent.* In a one-person operation, that wait can be substantial. Even though the occupancy rate is still low, the service level has already begun to erode.

Taken further, the occupancy rate of a one-person call center can be forced higher by driving more calls to it without increasing staffing. As such, callers pile up in queue, hold times mushroom, and the average answer time skyrockets. In short, the only way for a solitary agent to realize a high occupancy rate is to have calls continuously in queue, which produces poor customer service.

Although *it all depends* on many other factors, small call centers can generally only achieve average occupancy rate percentages in the mid-twenties to upper thirties. Attempting to push rates higher will result in a customer service disaster.

As call centers get larger, efficiencies increase and there are more agents available to handle calls in queue faster. Therefore, traffic spikes are easier to deal with as there are more available agents taking the calls. The midsize call center can experience occupancy rates at 50 percent, plus or minus.

Larger call centers, enjoying an even greater economy of scale, can respond better to traffic peaks and can therefore keep agents occupied a higher percentage of time while still maintaining an acceptable service level. Occupancy rates in the seventies become a realistic goal.

Last, it's the very large call centers—with hundreds of agents working simultaneously—that can experience call center delight. They can provide acceptable service levels even though their agents are chugging along at occupancy rates in the mid- to upper nineties.

All of this to indicate that, as far as the ideal occupancy rate goes, I can correctly say, "It all depends." I'm not being cavalier, merely honest.

Percent of Labor Costs

Another common area of interest is determining an appropriate percentage of expenses spent on labor. Here too, *it all depends*, with call center size being the primary variable. Again, starting with the smallest of call centers—one agent per shift—there's a potential for overhead to be low and therefore labor costs will be high. The person taking calls often also handles administrative and management tasks at slow times during the day (or night). As a result, all functions in the small call center can be highly integrated and efficient. This means low overhead. Therefore, the percent of expenses spent on labor can be around 50 to 70 percent.

When small call centers increase in size, more effort and expense go to expanding corporate, management, and control structures. Supervisors need to be added, customer service staff become necessary, an accounting function is separately identified, and so on. As a result, a much higher percentage of expenses is allocated to non-agent areas, and the percentage spent on labor correspondingly decreases. Mid-sized call centers can be the most inefficient, with labor percentages dropping below 50 percent.

For larger call centers, the support and organizational structure is cost-efficiently expandable to handle increased economies of scale. As a result, with the increased scope comes a decrease in the percentage of costs spent on nonoperational functions. This pushes the percent spent on labor back up. For the largest call centers, experiencing massive economies of scale, labor percentages rise to 70, 80, or even 90 percent because of all the other costs being spread over more and more agents. From a business standpoint, this is the most efficient and cost-effective call center scenario.

Synopsis

Given these two examples, you might conclude that larger call centers are ideal. After all, with increased size comes increased call occupancy rates and greater efficiency (that is, increased labor percentages and correspondingly decreased overhead).

There are, however, some downsides experienced in the larger call center: increased management and control issues, along with far greater complexity.

So, in determining what the ideal call center size is, I can unequivocally state, "It all depends."

Final Thoughts

Realize the danger in comparing call center metrics with different sized operations. The likelihood of misalignment and reaching wrong conclusions is high.

OPTIMIZING YOUR CALL CENTER
MAXIMIZE YOUR CALL CENTER EFFECTIVENESS THROUGH PEER COMPARISONS

North American culture salutes the solitary leader, the charismatic visionary, and the lone voice. It celebrates those who march with boldness to their own beat. This makes for exciting cinema, painting an inspirational picture for viewers to admire and emulate. It offers to fill that longing for distinction many people desire. Yet it isn't a proven path to success.

John Donne correctly stated, "No man is an island, entire of itself." King Solomon wrote, "A cord of three strands is not easily broken." It's true that there is safety in numbers.

Aside from socialization, human nature and pride prompt us to go it alone, to believe we can make superior decisions in a vacuum without the input of others. This is generally an unwise course.

Yes, examples exist of a solo individual who built a corporate empire, turned an inevitable military defeat into victory, or invented a product that changed the world. Unfortunately, for every well-publicized success story there are hundreds of quiet failures of people who tried to *do it my way* and flopped.

The proven formula for success is to surround yourself with talented advisors, faithful friends, and available mentors. It's through the wise counsel of many that the road to success opens, for if one falls, another is there to pick him or her up.

Although there are many ways to benefit from the valued support of others, two stand out for facilitating call center optimization. These are benchmarking and business improvement groups. While vastly different in both scope and direction, they share several basic traits.

First, they provide input from peers that can be used to inform your call center operation in comparison to theirs. This provides a baseline to determine areas of deficiency, as well as to celebrate operational success.

The second similarity is that they provide quantifiable results. They don't advance theoretical ideas, grandiose plat-itudes, or unrealizable goals. They provide real numbers from real businesses, thereby offering real solutions.

Third, once done, it's easy to repeat and update these efforts. This gives a timeline of successive snapshots of your operation, providing a regular report card showing your successes, your shortcomings, your improvements, and your relapses—all with respect to your peers.

One caution, however, is to avoid discussing pricing or anything that might be construed as price fixing or collusion.

Now that we know how benchmarking and business improvement groups are similar, let's discover what they are, how they are different, and practical steps to move forward. We'll address this in the next two chapters.

Final Thoughts

Benchmarking and business improvement groups are both valuable mechanisms to bring outside experience, knowledge, and results into a call center. With this input, business goals become more defined and realistic; direction, clearer; and focus, sharper.

BENCHMARKING

IMPROVE YOUR CALL CENTER OUTCOMES THROUGH INFORMATION SHARING

Benchmarking is the comparison of your business with statistical results from the norm of industry peers. These numeric measurements, called metrics, can be financial figures, sales numbers, operational quality, efficiency, human resource efficacy, or whatever the participants deem as most valuable. Typically, however, they are operational in nature.

Successful benchmarking follows a progressive path toward a desired outcome.

First, there must be a desire to obtain, have, and use the information.

Next, you need to determine who to invite to participate. The basic requirement is for participants to have an interest in the results and a commitment to contribute. Beyond that, it's imperative that all participants are in sufficiently similar business niches within a common industry. In many cases, it's wise to select those using a common call center platform. Operational metrics are hard to compare when their source comes from different systems with misaligned statistical standards.

The third step is to determine which numbers to measure or gather. In this regard, start small, obtaining only a few key numbers. As participants become engaged in the process and realize its value, add other metrics.

Follow this by developing how to gather information or make calculations. Without a standard methodology, each participant will make the calculation as they see fit, rendering any comparisons unreliable. These two steps can be both time consuming and contentious. Assistance from someone with experience in benchmarking or a background in statistical analysis is most helpful. This individual can simplify the process and save valuable time. Also, if this person does not have a direct stake in the results, they can more objectively guide the process.

The fifth step is critical. It's developing the survey form, which includes documenting the source or calculation of the data. Although this seems straightforward, it can doom benchmarking, as a less than ideal survey form will result in misanalysis or failure. Again, someone with experience in benchmarking or survey development will be helpful.

Then, regardless of the quality of the survey form, it's critical to test it. What may seem clear to those who developed and reviewed the form could cause confusion among those completing it. Therefore, conduct a small field test. Correct any problems uncovered in the test before giving the benchmark survey to all participants.

The next two steps are to gather the completed surveys and to compile the results. Concerns reside in who performs these two tasks. It's imperative that everyone trust this person. Assign this duty to someone not participating in, nor benefiting from, the benchmarking process.

The results of the benchmarking survey should only be presented in aggregate form and then only to those who responded. Protect the source of all individual answers. In some cases, eliminate sections that would effectively expose one or two members. Distribute the results, often along with analysis and a commentary to all who participated.

Although conducting a benchmarking study once is valuable, the real benefit comes from repeated studies over time. In doing so, follow up with those who participated to determine any problem areas needing correction or additional data to be collected. Make these changes and repeat the survey. Do this at least annually, possibly semiannually, quarterly, or even monthly as determined by the participants.

Summary of Steps for Benchmarking

- Possess a desire to obtain, have, and use the information.
- Decide who will be invited to participate.

- Determine which numbers to measure or gather.
- Develop a standard for how to make calculations.
- Design the survey form.
- Test the form and correct problems.
- Distribute the form.
- Gather the completed surveys.
- Compile the results of the collected surveys.
- Present the findings.
- Analyze and correct any problems for next time.
- Determine additional data to collect in future surveys.
- Repeat the process periodically (at least annually).

Examples of Benchmarking Metrics

Operational

- Percent of calls answered
- Average time to answer
- Percent of calls placed on hold
- Average hold time
- Occupancy (percent of time spent working)
- Average call duration
- Average wrap-up time
- Number of calls answered per month
- Amount of time spent on calls per month

- Schedule adherence

Sales and Marketing

- Number of sales made
- Average amount of sale
- Number of inquiries
- Closing ratios
- Source of leads

Human Resource

- Annual turnover rate
- Average employee (agent) tenure
- Cost to hire one new agent
- Cost to train one new agent
- Starting pay per hour
- Average hourly rate

Financial

- Percent of revenue spent on labor
- Percent of revenue spent on marketing promotions

- Percent of revenue spent on all sales and marketing efforts
- Profit margin

Final Thoughts

Call center benchmarking provides operations with quantifiable numbers to gauge success and identify areas needing improvement.

BUSINESS IMPROVEMENT GROUPS
TAKE BENCHMARKING TO THE NEXT LEVEL

B uilding on the benchmarking concept is the more intense and valuable business improvement group.

Business improvement groups, sometimes called profit clubs, also have as their basis a quantitative element. Typically, the primary focus is financial. Members in the group can also consider operational metrics, sales numbers, and human resource outcomes.

While benchmarking benefits from many participants, business improvement groups function best with smaller numbers. Four to six members are ideal. The group meets regularly to compare their financial reports, exploring ratios for different cost areas, profits or losses, and perhaps upper management compensation.

This delicate level of private disclosure doesn't happen easily. Screen and select participants with care to ensure compatibility and aligned business objectives. Everyone must strive to establish a rapport. Finally, they must be committed to the process and maintain strict confidentiality.

The Life Cycle of Business Improvement Groups

Be aware that business improvement groups have a life cycle. There is the start-up phase, establishing a rapport, mutual disclosure, decreased interest, and dissolution or coasting.

Start-up Phase

The start-up phase is critical for a successful group. It includes finding members, agreeing on the need for the group, and establishing basic rules. Once formed, do not add members, as this threatens to break the free flow of information and disrupt group dynamics.

Establish a Rapport

The next step is establishing a rapport. Although some of this will have been done in the start-up phase and may have existed prior to that, it needs to elevate.

Consider social activities to let members learn about each other in a safe environment. Alternately embark on a weekend team-building exercise. This often presents the group with an intense challenge which can only be successfully resolved through teamwork and mutual trust. Close personal bonds will result.

Certainly, group members can develop this connection without either of these optional exercises, but it is done so at the expense of time.

During the rapport step, fine-tune the group's rules and reach consensus.

Disclosure

The middle stage, mutual disclosure, may immediately follow establishing a rapport or build slowly. This stage is the objective of the group, where useful business data is shared, explored, and discussed. This phase can last for a year or as long as four to five. It's unusual for it to last much longer.

During this phase, some members may lose interest or develop diverging business goals and drop out of the group. When this occurs, it's tempting to add new members to maintain a workable group size. But resist this impulse as it will compromise the ongoing viability of the group.

Decreased Interest

Following the disclosure stage is decreased interest. Here member commitment declines. This could produce increased interpersonal tension, a loss of group cohesiveness, or decreased results. Some members will respond by dropping out of the group, but most will continue, if only for the sake of appearance.

Dissolution/Coasting

The final stage is dissolution or coasting.

Dissolution is when the group concurs that no substantial progress is being made or is apt to occur in the future. They stop all work and don't schedule any more meetings.

Coasting results when members continue to participate, though with less vigor and frequency. Alternately, the meetings deteriorate into a social gathering. The benefit of coasting is that the group is still loosely held together and can quickly resume their original function if the situation warrants.

The Process

The basis for a business improvement group is financial. Groups, however, can cover other items. Business improvement groups can add any metric, though it's common for the group to delve deeper into these numbers than is possible with benchmarking.

As business improvement groups progress, the agenda can (but doesn't have to) evolve to become more holistic, covering subjective issues such as hiring and firing, business strategies and marketing plans.

Close groups occasionally progress still farther, pursuing

cooperative buying initiatives, joint ventures, collective investment, or even business consolidation. Though rare, the rewards can be great. It's critical, however, to not form groups with this as a goal.

One Caution

A concern with business improvement groups, especially if it involves direct competitors, is the perception—whether real or imagined—of price-fixing and collusion. Therefore, exercise great care to avoid these areas of impropriety and illegality. Consult with an attorney to learn what specific activities and discussions to avoid.

Final Thoughts

Business improvement groups can produce valuable information, likely unavailable from any other source or at any cost. They do, however, take more effort to get started and require more time to maintain. Use the above information as a guide to launch your group.

CALL CENTER INNOVATION PROVIDES FRESH OPPORTUNITIES

DEVELOP A MINDSET OF ONGOING CHANGE TO PRODUCE MEANINGFUL RESULTS

Most call center managers want to see innovation in their call center. They yearn for new solutions to enhance quality and drive customer loyalty. These are lofty goals. And they're equally hard to realize.

In truth, connecting call center innovation with actionable outcomes presents a challenging situation. Therefore, instead of seeking big, revolutionary business overhauls, look for simpler ways to integrate innovation in the day-to-day operation of your call center. Each time an innovation opportunity presents itself, look for ways your call center can provide incremental change using the tools you already have.

Here are three considerations.

Enhance Existing Services

With each new opportunity that presents itself, consider how it can enhance what you're already doing. Simply look for new ways to do what you're currently accomplishing, only better.

For example, when voicemail first came on the scene, the industry assumed automated message taking would replace people. Yes, this did happen, and some visionaries built new businesses around the technology, but most operations adapted the technology to enhance what they were already doing.

Offer New Services

Another consideration when call center innovation presents itself is to consider what new services you could offer because of it.

This is what many outsource call centers did when voicemail came along. They continued offering their agent voice services as they always had. And they added a new service using voicemail technology. Voicemail didn't replace what they were doing. It added a new service.

Expand into New Areas

Sometimes an innovation can allow you to expand into another area. For in-house call centers it might mean serving another department or offering a new service to your company. For outsource call centers, this may allow you to diversify into new markets.

Final Thoughts

Call center innovation need not happen in huge, revolutionary jumps. We can better apply innovation as manageable tweaks on a consistent basis over time. This is the best and easiest way to find new opportunities for your call center.

IS YOUR CALL CENTER READY FOR ANYTHING?

HOW TO SURVIVE WHEN RECEIVING TWICE THE CALLS, HAVING HALF THE STAFF, OR BOTH

R unning a call center is hard, at least doing it right. Even under normal conditions, managers struggle to balance traffic and staffing levels while maintaining high quality and minimizing complaints.

But what happens when conditions aren't normal? If you're slammed with calls for an extended time, how will you fare? What happens if several agents can't make it in to work? What if the remote access portion of your system goes down, leaving your local staff to handle everything?

One solution is to ignore the risk and hope nothing abnormal ever happens. But eventually, something abnormal will occur. It might be a weather event, a natural disaster, or a manmade crisis.

Use your imagination. It's easy to see any number of events that could cause call traffic to spike or your staffing levels to drop. In fact, these both could happen at the same time. How well could your call center manage trying to handle twice the number of calls with half the staff?

Here are some ideas:

Multilocation

If the source of the problem that moves you from normal to not normal is local, having a multilocation call center is one easy solution—provided the other locations are far enough away to not have the same scenario affect them. Of course, this strains the other call centers in the network, but more locations with more agents to share the load reduces the negative impact.

Remote Workforce

Many call centers use some work-at-home agents, whereas others prefer all staff to work from one centralized location. Regardless, allowing staff to work from a remote location during a crisis is a key option to minimize the impact. This could provide options for staff unable to make it in to the office, as well as make it easier for staff not scheduled to log in and help.

Strategic Partners

Having multiple locations and allowing staff to work remotely are key solutions to deal with abnormal call center scenarios. These tactics, however, only go so far. To supplement these two approaches, outsource call centers can form strategic partnerships with other call centers to help during an emergency. But select a call center partner geographically distant from you. If you're on the coast, work with one who is inland. If you're in the north part of the country, find one in the south. If you're east, go west.

Vendor Solutions

Check with your vendor to see what disaster mitigation solutions they offer. They may be able to help you better handle an unusual call center situation. They could also recommend strategic partners for you to work with.

Outsourcing

If you're an in-house call center, you may want to arrange with an outsourcing call center to help during a crisis. And if you're an outsourcing call center, work with another outsourcing call center to help you.

Automate

Regardless of your paradigm to provide people to help people, sometimes automating portions of your call response will serve callers better than not answering their phone calls at all or making them endure an excessive wait in queue.

Final Thoughts

The key to make any of this work is planning. When call center work is normal—as normal as it ever will be—is the ideal time to pursue solutions for when normal goes away. Don't wait for a crisis to hit and then scramble for solutions.

Preparation today will help achieve success tomorrow, even under less-than-ideal situations. When disaster strikes, you'll be glad you have a plan to address it.

~

If you liked *Call Center Connections,* please leave a review online. Your review will help others discover this book so they can read it too.

ABOUT PETER LYLE DEHAAN

Peter Lyle DeHaan, PhD, is a full-time, career author. He's published dozens of books, hundreds of articles, and thousands of blog posts. He's a passionate wordsmith whose goal is to change the world one word at a time.

Starting in 2001, Peter has been the publisher and editor-in-chief of *Connections Magazine* and other publications covering the call center industry. Prior to that, Peter's lifetime of experience includes managing a multi-location call center, employment with a call center vendor, and serving as a call center consultant.

Learn more at PeterLyleDeHaan.com.

OTHER BOOKS BY PETER LYLE DEHAAN

For a complete, up-to-date list of Peter's books, go to PeterLyleDeHaan.com.

Call Center Success Series
Healthcare Call Center Essentials
How to Start a Telephone Answering Service

Sticky Series
Sticky Customer Service
Sticky Sales and Marketing
Sticky Leadership and Management
Sticky Living

Academic Research

The Telephone Answering Service Industry

Turning a Telephone Answering Service into a Call Center

Other Books

Successful Author FAQs